CRYSTAL HEALING FOR BEGINNERS

Introduction to Crystal Healing: Learn How to Achieve Higher Consciousness and Enhance Your Spiritual Balance with the Power of Crystals and Healing Stones

**By
Crystal Lee**

© Copyright 2018 by Crystal Lee All rights reserved.

The following eBook is reproduced below with the goal of providing information that is as accurate and reliable as possible. Regardless, purchasing this eBook can be seen as consent to the fact that both the publisher and the author of this book are in no way experts on the topics discussed within and that any recommendations or suggestions that are made herein are for entertainment purposes only. Professionals should be consulted as needed prior to undertaking any of the action endorsed herein.

This declaration is deemed fair and valid by both the American Bar Association and the Committee of Publishers Association and is legally binding throughout the United States.

Furthermore, the transmission, duplication or reproduction of any of the following work including specific information will be considered an illegal act irrespective of if it is done electronically or in print. This extends to creating a secondary or tertiary copy of the work or a recorded copy and is only allowed with an express written consent from the Publisher. All additional rights reserved.

The information in the following pages is broadly considered to be a truthful and accurate account of facts and as such any inattention, use, or misuse of the information in question by the reader will render any resulting actions solely under their purview. There are no scenarios in which the publisher or the original author of this work can be in any fashion deemed liable for any hardship or damages that may befall them after undertaking information described herein.

Additionally, the information in the following pages is intended only for informational purposes and should thus be thought of as universal. As befitting its nature, it is presented without assurance regarding its prolonged validity or interim quality. Trademarks that are mentioned are done without written consent and can in no way be considered an endorsement from the trademark holder.

TABLE OF CONTENTS

Introduction 1
Chapter 1 *Explaining Crystal Healing* 3
    The History of Crystal Healing 3
    What Is Crystal Healing Exactly? 4
    The Importance of Learning & Practicing Crystal Healing 6
    The Effects of Crystal Healing 7
Chapter 2 *Guidelines For Engaging In Crystal Healing* 10
    How to Feel the Energy of Crystals 10
    How to Cleanse Your Crystals 11
    How to Connect with Your Crystals 13
    How to Grid with Crystals 15
    How to Heal with Crystals 16
Chapter 3 *Crystal Index* 18
    What Crystals Do What 18
    What Forms of Crystals Do What? 45
Chapter 4 *Explaining Chakra Healing* 52
    What Are the Chakras? What Is the Kundalini? 52
    What Is a Kundalini Awakening? 53
    How Is Crystal Healing Connected with the Chakras? 55
    On Clearing, Aligning, and Balancing Your Chakras with Crystals 56
Chapter 5 *Other Methods Of Crystal Healing* 59
    On Subtle Energy 59
    Modalities of Crystal Healing 60
    Modalities of Subtle Energy Healing 68
    How to Incorporate Crystals into Any Modality 76
Chapter 6 *Advanced Crystal Healing And Details Of The Craft* 78
    Feminine or Masculine? 78
    Fire, Earth, Air, or Water? 80
    Solar System Associations? 81

What Goes Well with What?... 84
How to Create Healing Pouches... 86
Crystal Healing for the Zodiac.. 90

Conclusion 97
Description 98

INTRODUCTION

Welcome to *Crystal Healing for Beginners*. By downloading this book, you should consider yourself both lucky and blessed, for the contents that follow will surely change your world. Congratulations for the download and for beginning (or continuing) your adventure with healing crystals through this text in particular.

In the following pages, you'll be introduced to many aspects of crystal healing, but you'll start with the basics. In the first chapter, we explore the history of crystal healing and what it is exactly as well as its importance and the importance of *you* learning it. Finally, we'll examine the effects of crystal healing on the mind, body, emotions, and more.

In the second chapter, we get right into it with a set of guidelines and instructions to begin crystal healing in your own life. We'll practice how to feel the energy of our crystals and connect with them, how to cleanse them, how to create grids with them, and *then* how to explicitly heal with the assistance of crystals.

The third chapter is essentially an index of over one hundred stones, minerals, and crystals as well as a guide to which *types* – which *forms* – of crystals do what. For example, sometimes you'll be working with raw and rough crystals that perhaps you found yourself while most of the time, you'll likely be healing with imported and polished (or "tumbled") low-grade "gems," stones, and crystals instead. What *type* of crystal you have to use makes a relative difference in its energy, and the more you know, the more efficient your crystal healing abilities will become.

The fourth chapter provides the details of the chakras, kundalini, and how crystal healing relates to both. If you're coming to crystal healing hoping for assistance with awakening as well as general healing, this chapter will be right up your alley, for it will help you diagnose "disease" that lies in your chakras and that goes deeper than surface hurts. By connecting to your inner subtle energy vortexes in this way, you'll find yourself changed for the better in no time.

In the fifth chapter, we dive deeper into a discussion on what subtle energy is, how crystals affect it, what other modalities of divination and healing exist, and how to tie crystals into any of those modalities without issue. Finally, chapter six provides even more details on how crystal healing works as well as an introduction on how to pair or group crystals into healing pouches specifically designed for any one person, theme, or level of disease.

By the end of this book, you will have been flooded with important knowledge regarding crystal healing, and you will feel ready and excited to begin experimenting with it in your own life. You'll be surprised how soon it'll be *you* whose pockets jingle with the daily assortment of nature bits, small faceted crystals, and tumbled stones. Thank you for the download, and welcome!

CHAPTER 1
Explaining Crystal Healing

As we start off on our journey with crystal healing, we'll touch base on its origins and what it will mean for your life. While these tiny and tough nature bits look like they're just glorified paperweights, you might be surprised what potential they actually contain and how long that potential has been tapped into by our own humanoid ancestors.

The History of Crystal Healing

Humans have been using pieces of the earth as talismans and jewelry for as far back as we can study, essentially. Early beads were traded economically and were carved from bones, coral, and teeth of the animals our ancestors caught and ate to survive. From as long ago as 60,000 years, Russians made beads from mammoth tusks and buried them with their dead. As long as 30,000 years ago, amulets made from amber in the Baltic region were traded and made for fashion.

Early humans from as late as 10,000 years ago began to become increasingly skilled in their stone and gem trades. Around this time, Brits began trading amulets ever increasingly, using stones of amber, jet, rhyolite, and more. When the ancient Egyptians and Greeks came to the historical foreground, both cultures relied heavily on crystal accents for nobility and for high priests/priestesses. In fact, the word "crystal" itself comes from the ancient Greek word for "ice."

In addition, ancient Chinese peoples were fashioning incredible things, from beads to armor and masks out of jade, and the Scandinavian Vikings used translucent calcite to navigate across their narrow sea, enabling their Western raids on England, France, Italy, Africa, and more. In many religions, crystals were becoming considered holy and coveted possessions. In fact, Christianity around 350 AD had to ban the use of amulets in its followers, for crystal healing became increasingly associated with paganism and "unholy" earth worship around that time. For them, only the elite of the church was worthy and incorruptible by these nature bits' incredible powers.

In the Renaissance period, crystals were used a bit more and more frequently as cures for ailments, but only for upper nobility, and the rising and falling religions of the time made it hard to tell which rulers supported crystal healing and which didn't. The last thing you wanted was to recommend a gem cure to a staunchly pious ruler. During the Renaissance period, too, the "modern-day" study of crystal healing was officially established by a physician at the German court. In a time of increasing religious skepticism, this physician talked of good (or bad) angels working within the stones for (or against) healing, and the crowd (and the King) ate it right up. Since then, the onset of the Age of Enlightenment and Reason caused the crystals another fall from grace, but as the centuries and decades pass to now, crystals seem to be accepted *almost* more than ever for their healing capacities.

While it is true that gem and crystal healing has existed across time in varying degrees (starting with those earthen amulets and talismans of the past, leading up to the "sophisticated" attempts at gridding and crystal healing today), a new age dawns in terms of its appreciation. Starting in the '70s loosely and burgeoning widely in the 1980s, crystal healing has become something that straddles the line between a bonafide healing method and a hippie's placebo effect.

Regardless what you *think* of crystal healing, however, the physical and historical reality of the practice remains clear, and the resurgence today only proves that we're entering an age of increased energetic and vibrational sensitivity. We're entering a return to the feminine vibration, to the potential of subtle energy healing, and to the effects that crystals can have on us, and in this flooding-in feminine age, any tools the earth has to give us are both valid and life-altering. It comes down to us as to whether they're used and how much credit we give to our earth.

What Is Crystal Healing Exactly?

Crystal healing is a modality of subtle energy healing that relies on crystals, gems, minerals, and stones to make its point, and the point is fundamentally this; every carbon-based life-form has a vibrational expression, too, and that vibrational expression provides healing aid to others lacking in that vibration. For crystal healing, it's these rough and tough little nature bits pack quite the energetic punch when they're used and treated in the right ways.

Crystals can be used to give energy boosts and to calm people down, to attract what people want in life and to protect them from their worst fears, to enhance certain personality traits and to tone down unproductive ones, to heal physical ailments and alleviate pressure and pains, and so much more. Crystals, whether raw, polished, large, or small, are an underappreciated and influential healing modality.

To many inhabitants of today's world, the sound of a phrase like "crystals can make you feel better," in any capacity, will be received not as truth but as madness. For these people in this contemporary, highly scientific and technological world, it seems utterly impossible that a small chunk of earth can do anything but hold down paper. However, the millennia of crystal work before our time speaks to another type of truth; the truth of crystal healing. In fact, crystals are used today to store, transmute, and focus energy to make watches, ultrasound machines, lasers, certain surgeries, computers, and other numerous electronics, which goes to show that their value is hardly nil, even to the scientifically-minded.

Crystal healing works based on vibrations, frequencies, and resonances, but that doesn't mean it's all a bunch of hooey. Crystals and minerals can harness light and sound into beams of energy that a crystal practitioner can then direct for healing purposes. Sometimes, it is the metal within a stone that helps, creates, or amplifies its healing vibration, such as with malachite and its copper contents. Sometimes, it is the location the crystal or mineral was mined or harvested from. Sometimes, it is the stone's positive or negative electric charge. Sometimes, it's the dye the crystal's powder creates and those connotations, and sometimes, it's even the crystal's power that aids with (physical & emotional) troubles within.

When it comes to crystal healing with complexes of disease and chronic illness, those vibrations and qualities of remedy that naturally exist within each mineral can be used to both treat symptoms of the disease and, at times, mitigate its presence altogether. Ancient Chinese people found that jade worked to mitigate kidney ailments millennia ago, and shamans of many cultures seem to have realized the crystals' harnessing power and then used it to their tribes' advantages. Crystal healers today are just tapping into this ancient tradition with renewed vigor, and each individual's practice makes the collective smarter and stronger, without us ever physically communicating.

The Importance of Learning & Practicing Crystal Healing

It makes a lot of sense that so many people would be drawn to crystal healing at this time in earth's present history. The earth is experiencing a period of great turmoil. Regardless of what you call it and why you think it happened, the earth's temperatures are increasing, and our planet is heating up. Our winters are becoming colder and fiercer too. The magnetic poles are shifting, and those temperature extremes are amplifying, just like watching a young child being pushed on a swing by a powerful adult. The tips of the pendulum arc become higher and higher, more and more extreme by the minute.

Not only is our earth going through menopause, basically, but our cultures are going through great strife, with an increased desire to separate rather than join forces together. War is as prevalent as ever, and it exists for as exploitative reasons as ever. Hunger and famine and poverty reign in certain parts of the world. Humans are in almost constant conflict, it seems, with one another, animals, and the earth itself. Even the very crystals we use for our healing have been taken harshly from the earth, but now that they're extracted, it's up to us to send back love, solidarity, respect, and healing straight to that earthen source.

So many people are coming to crystal healing now because we and our planet so desperately need it. We need to return to the power of collective healing, even if it happens first on an individual level. We need to remember the power of the earth, and what better way to do that than to work with her gorgeous nature bits and amplify love right back to their source. Being alive on this planet at this time grants us a huge responsibility. Either we live freely and unconsciously exploit the earth and plunder resources to the detriment of humanity's future, or we choose to live consciously and righteously in partnership with the earth, promising to give love where love has always been due in exchange for this powerful healing potential.

You are being called to crystal healing for a reason. Whether it's to heal yourself, someone close to you, or a group of people in the future, you're fascinated by these incredible earthen materials so that you'll remember your origin and feel connected to a divine purpose. No matter what healing work you're here for, you're sure to be blown away by the potential of your relationship with these crystals in no time.

The Effects of Crystal Healing

Crystal healing's effects on the human body, mind, and soul, are too numerous to just list outright, so it will be helpful in this case to divide our approach to discuss the multiple benefits of crystal healing in terms of *where* the effect will be housed. We'll start with the effects on the mind and mental faculties before moving onto the physical body and human physiology generally. Then, we'll discuss how crystals can affect emotions and emotional health before ending with their abilities to build and focus one's personal power toward a variety of ends.

...On the Mind

As far as the effects of this healing modality on the mind go, they are both numerous and highly beneficial. Having certain crystals and minerals around, in whatever form, can increase the individual or group's focus, creativity, organization, productivity, clear communication, psychic abilities, multitasking capacity, abilities to attract love and a romantic partner, abilities to attract wealth, abilities to protect one's home, and abilities to protect from pollution (environmentally and technologically). It can also help the individual clear unproductive thought cycles, it can give a boost to one's intellect, and it can help one work through destructive personality traits to the other side where things are decidedly a bit less harsh.

...On the Body

As far as the effects of this healing modality on the body go, they can do so much it's almost innumerable. Crystals can help with any of the ailments that follow: degenerative brain disorders, cancer, addiction or drug dependency, respiratory problems, blood pressure issues, blood sugar issues, diabetes, circulatory problems, heart defects, joint pain or insecurity, general pain and back pain, headaches and migraines, broken bones, strained muscles, tired or diseased eyes and vision, sore throat, asthma constrictions, infections (whether bacterial or fungal, in any part of the body), autoimmune disorders, depressive neurotransmitter imbalances, infertility, menstruation and menopause, nutritional absorption issues, digestive issues, and general inflammation.

...On Emotions

As far as the effects of this healing modality on one's emotions go, they're so positive and numerous that it's comforting to even consider. For people struggling with breaking a habit, loss and grief, depression, manic-depressive tendencies or bipolar disorder, broken heart, anxiety or stress-related chronic illnesses, panic attacks, feelings of being unlovable, feelings of listlessness and purposelessness, and even feelings of unworthiness, crystals can be an incredible aid through both their potential to comfort generally, as a weight in one's hand, and to mitigate the physiological responses that feed into some emotional complexes. For people seeking peace, calm, solace, mental balance, emotional clarity, anger management, and help with defensiveness, crystals can also be an incredible boon through just their presence, if not, then with their presence *applied* to healing.

...On Your Personal Power

As far as the effects of this healing modality on your personal power will go, I almost don't want to tell you so that you can be pleasantly surprised. I'll let you know a good bit of what's in store for you, at least. As you reconnect with your personal power through crystal healing, you'll come to realize that is it your *relationship* of working with the stones that make things happen in your life, and you'll come to reconnect with yourself. You might find that you become connected to yourself through past life visions too, for a handful of minerals and crystals even listed in this book have the abilities to connect you in that way. You might also find that you have the potential to make a connection with your spirit guides or surrounding angels and that potential is almost inexplicably enormous.

You might finally find that you grow in strength and capacity through your application of crystal healing in a way that brings you confidence. You may find a connection with your personal power through your voice, your assertiveness, and your abilities to live out your life the way that best suits *you*. Essentially, crystal healing has several effects on the body, mind, and soul, but perhaps none are so moving and influential as its ability to connect you with the best version of yourself in real time. Just wait and see what you can make happen.

CHAPTER 2
Guidelines For Engaging In Crystal Healing

Before just jump right into crystal healing, step back and take it all in. It might seem like a lot, but you still have a long way to go. You'll have to learn the essentials – the intricate inner workings of crystal healing – to see what you're in for before you decide if it's right for you*.

* Spoiler Alert: If you've made it this far, it's probably right for you!
*

How to Feel the Energy of Crystals

As someone who may be just getting started with crystal healing, you likely need an introduction on where to even begin. That's absolutely understandable, and you needn't worry. I'll walk you through exactly what to do to begin your incredible and healing relationship with these wondrous little nature bits. We'll start with just feeling the energy of the crystals and getting in touch with them in that way before going all the way into the use of them for healing. After feeling things out, we'll learn about cleansing, programming one's intentions, gridding, and *then*, finally, healing.

If you've ever been given a crystal before, or if you've had one or two random ones since you were young for no reason, go find those stones! If you definitely have never been gifted one, and you're certain you have none, go out to a metaphysical or mineral store and pick out just one or two to start. Once you have your starter minerals and crystals gathered, it's time to try closing your eyes and getting better attuned with the stones' inner vibrations.

The following exercise can be used on any mineral or crystal to help you feel connected to its energy and get a sense of its nature. This exercise can also be used to connect with the vibrational essences of plants, trees, herbs, flowers, and more, so don't be afraid to use this technique for any form of healing and knowledge gathering. It can take you farther than you know. The exercise is essentially this; holding the stones, you'll close your eyes and quiet your mind of excess thought, waiting to feel the vibration of the stone in your hand. If you're extra patient, you may even be able to intuit its healing capacity, too.

Meditating is a crucial part of how one can better feel the energy of crystals. The ability to close one's eyes and close out the world, to a certain degree, is immensely helpful when attuning to the vibration of a stone so small it fits, perhaps, on your thumbnail. By quieting the noise of the world and the chatter of the mind, the individual can learn to sense those quiet things that normally go so unnoticed. Like the glistening path of a snail on the sidewalk or the chirp of a cardinal, the vibrational essence of a crystal is small, but to some, it can be loud. To those who have trained themselves to silence out the unnecessary, even these small gestures can mean healing.

With your eyes closed, then, and the stone or stones in your hand, try to feel out the essence. You might feel it in terms of an amplified heartbeat under the crystal or a muscle spasm. You might feel it in terms of relaxation in your one arm or overall peace and satisfaction. Simply be calm and quiet; breathe and be still, and just wait to see what surfaces. Breathe evenly and deeply and take in this moment with this crystal. If any distracting thoughts or emotions or urges enter your mind, simply breathe them in or blow them away like smoke or fog or clouds.

As you meditate with the stone in your hand and begin to feel its vibration, make note of how it makes you feel. Make note of its effects, too; you could even keep a crystal journal if you like doing that sort of thing, and you can keep more detailed notes about your experiences and occurrences with each stone. After a little while, you will likely feel encouraged to carry certain crystals with you throughout the day, whether placed in your car, your pocket, your purse, or otherwise. And then, you can note the differences of how the crystal affects your *day*, rather than just how its vibration feels in your hand. With a crystal in your pocket, you're well on your way to learning and actualizing the full and potential intricacies of crystal healing in your life.

How to Cleanse Your Crystals

Crystals can take on a lot of energetic weight as you begin to work with them more and more. Even with one just sitting in your hand or being carried through the day in your pocket, it can pick up certain things from you and hold onto them until you help it find its release. Some crystals can cleanse themselves and won't need you. For example, selenite, quartz, and carnelian are excellent self-cleansers, and they're so strong they can clear the energies of any others they're near.

However, other stones are not so low-maintenance, and for those crystals and minerals, the following guide will become imminently helpful. As far as when to cleanse your crystals goes, you'll want to do it if or when any of the following 10 things happen: (1) you've just used the crystal, (2) you're just about to use it after a long time of it sitting, (3) someone else handled your crystal, especially if you don't trust or like that person, (4) someone else used the crystal to heal him or herself, (5) you think the crystal was mistreated or misused in some way, (6) you or someone else brought intense negative energy around the crystal, (7) it actually looks dirty or feels sticky, (8) you're preparing for a special ritual, (9) something major has changed for you/in your life, or (10) you're using a crystal you normally use for yourself on someone else.

If your crystals are polished, the easiest and most stress-free method is to put them under running water. You can choose to use sink water, poured spring or filtered water, naturally-running spring or creek water, still lake water, or even puddle water for this task, but the most ideal would be to find a natural source of running water and take your crystals there for a cleansing ritual. Be careful when using even polished versions of calcites and malachite for this type of cleansing, however, for the copper in malachite will become dull and the exterior of the calcite will begin to dissolve. Use these types of stones for the following method instead.

If your crystals are raw or in crystalline form, you'll want to try something different. You could always lay these crystals out on a selenite sheet or slab, or you could lay them onto the points of a quartz cluster. You could also put them onto a plate (or inside an opaque bag) with a piece or two of carnelian. However, the best method for crystals of this nature will always be to bathe them in the moonlight. Crystals that are raw and flaky are called friable, and these often dissolve in water and drastically fade (color-wise) in daylight. In order to protect crystals of this nature and other sensitive raw ones, choose moonlight as your cleanser and charger. Full moonlight is always best, but any night when the moon is out can work for a moment of cleansing. Just lay your crystals out in view of the moon, and the rest is up to nature.

If you'd like to try something different, there are a variety of other options at your disposal as well. Generally, you can apply the conditions you already listed. You can set any stone in running water (based on its physical qualities) or even a bowl of water for cleansing. You can set any stone in a pouch with another cleansing crystal, or you can set the stone on a cluster of cleansing crystals instead. You can use moonlight, as with friable, raw, and sensitive stones and minerals, and then the fun begins.

You can also use techniques for cleansing your crystals that involve other minerals, such as salt or soil. You can bury any stone, mineral, or crystal into a bowl of salt or soil to cleanse it from any energetic intensity. Furthermore, you can use indirect techniques of bathing your crystals in sunlight (be careful with amethysts though, they might fade!) or in an energetic shield of visualization on your behalf. Through meditation, you can visualize any amount and degree of cleansing any crystal may desire. Finally, you can use the "more direct" indirect means of cleansing, as through sound and incense smoke. The sonorous sound of a struck singing bowl, gong, bell, or chime can cleanse and refocus the energy of a crystal, and the smoke of an incense stick, as well as the smudge smoke from both sage and palo santo, can do the same.

How to Connect with Your Crystals

When it comes to connecting with your crystals after they're cleansed and ready to go, your relationship will be entirely changed. You won't be protecting, cleaning, and almost coddling the stone back to its healthiest, purest state of being; it will be time to put things into focus. It will be time to program your crystals with your specific healing intention, and while that may sound like a daunting task, I promise, it's easier than it sounds, and it will become second nature in no time.

As you learned when you sat and felt the vibration of the crystals a few sections ago, some crystals have a specific healing goal in mind, and with the right application of intuition, you can tell what the crystal *wants* to do. When you sit with your cleansed crystal now, how does its vibration feel? Was it affected by the cleansing, or does it largely feel the same? Is there anything worthy of note in your crystal journal? Most importantly, does it feel like the crystal wants to do any sort of work in particular? When you sit and meditatively feel that vibration, do you receive answers of this nature? If so, follow up with that direction. If not, provide your own.

If it comes down to providing your own direction and healing intention, the best way to "program" your crystal with that information is as follows. First, cleanse the space you're sharing with the crystal. You want to make sure that the environment you're inhabiting doesn't imprint any distracting energies onto the crystal while you're attempting this work, and you also want to make sure that any lingering energies of anyone else who's entered the space don't get attached to the crystal instead of or before your own. Smudge the room with sage or palo santo smoke to accomplish this feat.

Second, set all electronic devices out of the room completely. Get any distracting electromagnetic radiation and pollution out of the space so the crystal doesn't get too focused on something that's not you right off the bat. Third, hold the crystal in your hand and begin to meditate. Imagine what you want the crystal to do. Visualize that potential if you can. Really imagine it with detail. See the outcome, the circumstances that would lead up to it, and its resolution. See the togetherness and the community. See the success and achievement. Whatever you're hoping for, visualize it with this crystal held gently but with purpose.

Fourth and finally, breathe in all that intention, open your eyes, and exhale, blowing out your intentions and goals onto the crystal itself. Imagine that your goals are getting physically stuck to the crystal and that the crystal will want to work to solve or actualize those dreams in order to clear itself and get back to its most natural state. Visualize that the crystal is grateful for the task, and make sure to express your own sense of gratitude for the crystal's work, too. The more respected the subtle energy of the crystal is, the better its work will turn out. It might sound crazy, but it's true: the purer and kinder the approach, the better this technique will work overall.

How to Grid with Crystals

When it comes to crystal healing, one of the most effective and impactful methods is to set up a grid and then place your intention and energizing abilities onto that specific crystal set up. As you continue learning about minerals and what crystals work well together (and then when you read through the final chapter of this book and start thinking explicitly about crystal pairings and groupings), it will become obvious to you how one's healing intentions can be strengthened when several minerals are used that can work together for the same purpose.

Until you get to this point, it will suffice to know that grids are setups of crystals that usually involve two or more types of crystals (for example, the two types could be amethyst and rose quartz) which are then attuned to work together (whether naturally, intentionally, or both) to achieve a specific healing goal. Once it's agreed on what type of healing will be done and what crystals will be used, the individual can then plan what the grid itself will look like and what format is best for the style of healing in question.

Sometimes, the healing project deals with individual struggles, physiological alterations, or personality adjustments. In these cases, it's appropriate to formulate the grid *around the individual in question* so that the crystals' energies work together directly in relation to that person. Sometimes, the grid can even be established around the individual's workspace, bedroom, bed, or office so that the maximum effect can be achieved through a long-standing setup.

Sometimes, the healing project deals with altering the energies of environments or physical spaces. For these healing goals, it would be best to set the grid up around the edges of the space in question. If it's a natural space like a park, set up a few stones all the way around the park's perimeter if you can. If it's a room, grid the border, and if it's a home, you can even make a grid outside the residence with stones.

Sometimes still, the project involves healing a group of people. In this case, the grid would be a little more complicated and you have two main options. First, you can set up a stationary grid in your home that represents everyone involved, with a crystal or two focused on healing each person. Second, you can give each person a few stones from the grid to carry on them always, and as the individuals move about the world, the shape of the grid will change, giving everyone a transformative and interactive healing experience.

A few, more specific, guides to crystal gridding can be found in chapter 5. If you're really fascinated by this concept, flip forward, for basic grids to benefit those experiencing heartbreak, recent home invasion or feelings of insecurity and household unsafety, excessive stress, chakra imbalance, and (auto-)immune problems are included when other modalities of crystal healing are discussed in this later chapter.

How to Heal with Crystals

After you've set your intention with the crystal's approval and meditatively connected your energies in that way, you'll have to move forward. However, you might be at the point where you haven't even chosen the crystal for the task yet, and clearly, that's the place to start. If this situation describes yours, you can try several different techniques to choose the right crystal for you.

First, you could just go to a mineral store (whether online or in person) and intuitively choose a crystal without doing any research and then begin your work with it when it arrives at your home. Second, you could do research based on what ailments you want to heal, choose the right stones respectively, and then put them to action. Third and finally, you could do research based on a stone you're drawn to and then use it regardless of its healing capacities because you know it will benefit you somehow.

Regardless of what method you use, choose your stone or stones and prepare them for healing. Cleanse them, connect with them, and set your intention after doing your choosing and research. Then comes the good stuff. At this point, you'll have to energize your crystal so that it has all the power it needs to do that good work you asked it to do (and technically, you can do this energizing step before you complete the intentional programming, depending on how things play out; it doesn't matter *too* much the order here).

A few different ways you can energize your crystal, stone, or mineral include using water, moonlight, sunlight, or physical contact with the hands (or inflicted body part) of the person in need of healing. Energizing with water would involve sitting your stone in running water if able, or in a bowl of water if it's too sensitive. If it's too sensitive for water contact whatsoever, you can put the stone next to a glass of water in the sunlight or in an enclosed jar that's immersed in water.

Energizing with moonlight or sunlight involves using those natural light energies to give a boost to the potential of the stone in question. Use indirect sunlight for light-colored stones, as they may fade in direct light. Finally, energizing with physical contact reflects on an ancient Native American tradition, whereby nothing was used to amplify the potential of a stone other than the hands of the person it would be used to heal. Connecting one's energy with the stone in this way can be exactly what the crystal's essence needs to link with you for the future work of healing.

Finally, you'll want to consider where you'll put the stone or crystal when it comes down to that healing work. Certain placements work better than others, especially depending on the theme of the healing. Are you working for protection? Make a grid in your home or set stones right inside the doorway. Are you working to heal one of your organs? Find a way to hold that stone with you daily and keep it as near to that organ as possible. Are you working to clear the energy of a room or set of rooms? Make a gem essence (see chapter 5) and spritz it into the room out of a spray bottle whenever help is needed. Overall, placements to consider are nearby or on the person in question, in the room, in a spray bottle for the room, in the home (as inside main doorways), on a prayer altar, or worm in pockets or as jewelry.

CHAPTER 3
Crystal Index

This chapter will become your best friend as you continue building your relationship with these little, powerful nature bits. Eventually, you may use this chapter as a go-to for finding out what healing crystals and stones do what. The following pages delineate over 100 crystals and their abilities for aiding and manifesting metaphysical learning, spiritual development, personal transformation, financial abundance, and more.

After the general index of crystal details, you'll find another section that addresses the formations of these special stones. This section will become as important to you as the extensive beginning section of this chapter, for the form of crystals or stones affects and *enhances* their abilities even to an exponential degree at times. In time, you'll realize what the difference is between an Amethyst geode and a piece of polished Red Jasper.

What Crystals Do What

A

Agate

Any form of this stone is notable for its peculiar repeated pattern. Usually, there are banded layers of internal forms within the stone that help you tell which form of agate is which. For instance, blue lace agate produces a pattern within that looks like white lace on a pale blue background, while moss agate varies in color but looks like it contains moss on the inside when polished. Generally, agates are good for protection and attracting luck and wealth. They're essential for earth healing and training with strength or endurance.

Blue Lace Agate works with the throat chakra and third eye chakra. It encourages kind and compassionate communication of one's truth as well as peace and wisdom, generally.

Fire Agate grounds and inspires its holder or wearer while protecting them fiercely. It ignites passion as well as personal awareness of one's soul mission, life purpose, or ultimate adventure.

Moss Agate stabilizes and reinvigorates one's energy, based on what one needs. It is especially attuned to earthwork and earth-related healing. It's also a great stone for self-esteem, as it boosts self-compassion and capacity for self-love even when times are tough.

Tree Agate provides a deep sense of inner calm and rejuvenates one's connection to the natural world. It also fights stagnation if you're having trouble with laziness or procrastination.

Amazonite

This crystal helps one feel at peace and works in support of the throat and heart chakras. It helps your self-expression be as genuine and heartfelt as possible, especially during times of great stress. It encourages an overall return to health and mental well-being.

Amethyst

This stone works for so many different things. It's a pain reliever, a psychic awakener, a sleep aid, a health booster, an energizer, and more. It's also incredibly helpful for meditation and finding one's truth despite hard times or trauma.

Chevron Amethyst helps to attune one's intuition and generally opens the third eye when applied in meditation. It also works to cleanse and heal subtle energy injuries and aura wounds.

Vera Cruz Amethyst, in particular, brings about good mood and reminds of the importance of play.

Apatite

Apatite helps reduce feelings of hunger while encouraging mental and emotional creativity. It boosts intellect, clairvoyance, confidence, and clarity.

Apophyllite

This crystal helps people who struggle with allergies as well as those who want a stronger connection to the spiritual side of things. In addition, apophyllite helps one perceive and act on their truth. For those skilled with meditation, apophyllite has the ability to open portals through space and time.

B

Beryl

This stone lets one release emotional baggage that may have been accumulating. It also helps one reach his or her greatest potential while encouraging their solar plexus and crown chakras to open. Beryl is also a powerful stress reliever that works for the circulatory system generally. It even fights infections in the body and issues with digestion.

Bloodstone

This green and red stone help with any issues related to blood, the heart, and circulation. It also connects its wearer or holder to their root and heart chakras for healing purposes. It grounds and centers as well as encourages devoted friendships and lasting loves.

Boji Stone

Boji stones are some of the best grounding stones, for they even help to root their holder in the present moment despite over-stimulation or stress. They help strengthen one's connection to earth generally, and they help one get over hurtful situations or lingering emotional wounds. Healing-wise, boji stones work well for pain relief and even tissue regeneration. They work best in pairs.

C

Calcite

Found in a wide variety of colors, calcite works with chakras of almost any color, too. Furthermore, it allows the release of stress and fear while invoking happiness and laughter to fill their places. Calcites are also generally good energy amplifiers.

Blue Calcite helps reduce blood pressure and relieve pain. It also dissolves energy blockages for the best possible recuperation and recovery.

Green Calcite allows one to release old habits without detriment to the mind or soul. It helps one "cut out the fat," so to speak, of his or her life and personality.

Orange Calcite promotes happiness and joy while providing healing power to the reproductive and digestive systems.

Yellow (or Gold) Calcite banishes negative energies surrounding the individual and heightens the experience of meditation.

Carnelian

This stone provides healing and balance for the sacral and solar plexus chakras while restoring one's overall energy and cleansing any stones or crystals near to it. Carnelian protects and draws abundance when placed inside the front door of one's home, too. It boosts energy, encourages interest and love of life, and helps with kidney disorders.

Chrysocolla

This stone heals the heart and throat chakras while relieving deep physical and psychological pains related to past trauma. It helps build one's strength and vitality to be able to grow past those hurts.

Citrine

Crystals of citrine are powerful attractors of abundance. They also enhance one's communication abilities while making him or her more decisive and confident. Citrine also helps boost creativity while clearing any negativity in the space or individual. Use these crystals for sacral or solar plexus healing.

D

Danburite

This crystal helps for those who need a self-acceptance boost. It works well for people who need help accepting others, too. It creates the sensation of lasting peace for the holder or wearer, despite any lingering emotional pain (no matter how deeply it's hiding). It is intimately connected to the heart chakra.

Diamond

As the hardest gemstones on Earth, diamonds encourage resilience, endurance, trust, and constancy along with everlasting love. Even rough diamonds can strengthen your energy field.

Dolomite

Dolomite harmonizes energies within any shared field, and it helps to release great sorrow. Athletes can use the stone for increased strength and stamina, while writers and artists can use it for boosted creativity and frequency of insightful thoughts.

Dumortierite

This crystal is the best stone for work on patience. It helps increase intuition and insight as it activates the third eye chakra, and for the physical body, it heals pains, diarrhea, and various intestinal problems. If you're having trouble choosing something or deciding what to do in life, this stone will be of great help to you, too.

E

Emerald

Emerald is a stone of the goddess that aligns with the heart chakra. Furthermore, it works to attract peace and harmony in one's life. For the physical body, emerald helps to heal eyesight, the heart, and the immune system.

Epidote

This crystal helps increase contact with entities outside this dimension and planet. It's a vibrational and energetic amplifier in that sense. Epidote also relieves feelings of depression and hopefulness by raising one's vibration to new potential (that was always the true potential in the first place).

Eudialyte

Eudialyte is particularly gifted when it comes to healing a broken heart, as it clears up negative energy build-up from something like a break-up or loss. It generally replaces negative feelings towards others with more positive, beneficial ones. Finally, this crystal clears out old, stagnant, unhelpful energy from the root, sacral, and heart chakras (even energy as old as would linger from a childhood trauma).

F

Fairy Stone

Fairy stones are naturally occurring calcium deposits, but they're also undeniably, energetically strong because of it. They help establish strong bones or strengthen weak ones, they make the skin stronger and more resilient, they help individuals cut bad habits completely, they relieve tensions or pain from radiation or chemotherapy, and they boost happiness and connectivity to nature.

Feldspar

Feldspar is almost unmatched in its abilities to trigger and enhance creativity, but it also helps you achieve standard goals through a simple boost of productively creative thinking. Feldspar helps you become more self-aware, too, while increasing self-acceptance and feelings of self-worth. It will essentially allow you to feel grounded and loving to all through your own experience of self-love.

Fluorite

This semi-transparent crystal comes in a variety of colors, but it always packs the same punch: it enhances focus, mental clarity, memory capacity, and organizational productivity. Furthermore, fluorite helps broaden one's mind and acceptance of others while protecting against viral infection.

Fulgurite

Through prayer, manifestation goals become immediate and material with the aid of fulgurite. They're stones of purification that help clear out what's unproductive in order to make way for larger, more impactful experience, not excluding one's own psychic/soul awakening.

Fuchsite

Fuchsite helps clear blockages on all levels while recreating balance and tranquility within once that clearing work is complete. It's an energetic amplifier of other crystals, and it also triggers a deep and lasting sense of compassion and understanding for others.

Fuchsite with Ruby works specifically to heal one's own heart and dissolve blockages of energy there. It opens the individual up, psychically, once that heart chakra work is finished.

G

Galena

This harmony stone helps reduce inflammation while stimulating the circulatory system. It works well to increase or maintain hair growth and helps the body absorb its necessary nutrients. It encourages safe intellectual exploration, too.

Galaxite

This stone is wonderful for dissolving stress and for healing conditions or illnesses related to the experiences or stress or chronic anxiety. For those with brain disorders, galaxite helps limit degeneration and backward progress. Finally, this stone works to aid digestion and boost metabolism while creating a lasting sense of peace and calm with one's life.

Garnet

This root chakra crystal is one of the most powerful energy boosters. When you're having a low day, grab a garnet! It also promotes overall health and attracts spice for your love life (or a love life in the first place, if that's where you find yourself starting from). Finally, garnet helps one access higher states of consciousness as well as the pain relief and blood healing one desires.

Gaspeite

This crystal is a powerful and impacting healer that maintains a healing vibration no matter how much negativity it happens to pick up. All the while, it imparts that healing vibration onto its holder or wearer, as well as that person's surroundings. It grounds you while opening your eyes, providing a spiritual perspective of any situation you encounter.

Gold

Gold works metaphysically to heal feelings of impurity, unworthiness, and general negativity. It encourages belief in one's inner strength and all the while attracts abundance.

Goldstone

This human-made stone glimmers with potential and it imparts that energy onto you too. Goldstone helps boost your life force energy, which you can call chi, prana, etc. Because it contains copper, it helps heal the circulatory system while easing inflammation of many types. It's also great for detoxification and strength building.

Green Aventurine

This stone is great for comfort and general healing assistance, but particularly for the heart, green aventurine provides incredible healing potential. It harmonizes the heart chakra while protecting the physical heart from a relapse into disease once healed. This stone can also settle feelings of nausea, disorder, and distress.

H

Heliodor

A great crystal for leaders and leadership, heliodor ignites charisma and inspired work. It will draw towards you such wonderful traits as confidence, self-awareness, group-awareness, assertiveness, decisiveness, and wisdom. If others come to you often with intention of manipulation, heliodor can help you see through their falseness while boosting your strength to shut them down.

Hematite

This metallic stone activates the root chakra while enhancing feelings of groundedness. It helps one find a balance between their masculine and feminine aspects as well. For those with blood issues, hematite will be a necessary companion.

Herkimer Diamond

These "diamonds" are actually a variety of quartz that aligns with the crown and third eye chakras. They increase dream activity and dream recall while grounding people who are often too "fiery." They clear all chakras, too, when used for chakra healing and meditations, helping the individual reach their highest possible potential (through clairvoyance, clairaudience, dream insights, and more).

Howlite

Howlite is a calming stone that strengthens manifestation abilities, reduces experiences of insomnia, connects one with wisdom and true insight, redirects anger sent your way, and helps dissolve triggers of any kind. Furthermore, this stone will work to balance calcium levels in the body for the benefit of one's overall health.

Blue Howlite, in particular, works well with sleep and dreaming. It increases abilities to fall asleep easily and stay asleep deeper, but it also aids in dream recall while enhancing your ability to process and interpret those dreams.

I

Infinite

This crystal works wonders for pain relief, both physical and emotional, but it also helps one process where those pains came from and what they mean for the past, present, and future. It also gradually increases one's capacities of dealing with others, other energies, and external stresses (especially for those people who are highly sensitive or empathic).

Iolite

Like hematite, iolite helps one find balance between his or her masculine and feminine features, aspects, traits, etc. In this way, iolite helps one find self-acceptance on a whole new level. Additionally, this crystal increases one's abilities of intuition and imagination while dissolving any emotional baggage that keeps the individual from feeling like he or she can handle the responsibility of any sort. Iolite can also promote psychic visions and crown, third eye, and throat chakra cleansing and alignment.

J

Jade

Jade works to promote many things. First of all, it aligns with the heart chakra to trigger feelings of love, wisdom, courage, and even mercy. Second, it works for overall good health and will help you live a good life. Third, it boosts strength, fertility, immunity, and more. Fourth and finally, jade can encourage the integration of healthy coping mechanisms in replacement of those that have failed or become unhealthy.

Jasper

Jasper generally works well for protection, earth connectivity, grounding, and overall health.

Basanite is technically a black jasper that can take you far away into altered states of consciousness along the lines of dreamwork and prophecy.

Blue Jasper also connects the individual to spiritual realms. It provides lasting energy during trying times, too, and it fights degenerative disease.

Brown Jasper heals examples of environmental stress, both on the individual and on the environment. It connects the individual to past lives in order to help heal as a whole being alongside the Earth. Finally, brown jasper has the potential to regenerate organ and immune health.

Green Jasper connects with the energy of the goddess while bringing your attention back to those things that have brought you joy in the past. It works well to heal skin disorders, to reduce inflammation generally, and to detoxify specifically and generally.

Mookaite, or Australian Jasper, is a great stone for couples, for it helps one see all sides of a situation before acting. Furthermore, it stabilizes and grounds the individual while purifying the blood, fighting infection, and healing a variety of wounds.

Orbicular Jasper demonstrates a circular pattern in its coloring, and it works to help those who work in the service of others maintain patience, respect, and individuality. Furthermore, it heals respiration, circulation, and systems of detoxification.

Picture Jasper conveys messages from the Earth to its children, all of animal-kind (including humanity). It helps us learn from past and present mistakes to heal the future, and it can kickstart a weakened immune system.

Purple Jasper works well with the crown chakra by reducing hypocrisy and unintentional (or intentional!) self-contradiction.

Red Jasper is the so-called "worry stone" that anxious, stressed-out, or worrisome people should carry with them always. It grounds, provides energy, increases insight, and stabilizes the body. Furthermore, it works to the benefit of one's liver, blood, and bile ducts.

Yellow Jasper works as a protector during travel of many sorts, and it can help one travel to spiritual realms, too. It aligns with the solar plexus chakra, so its effects heal digestion, the stomach, and the toxins that float around inside.

Jet

This stark black stone helps heal and reverse disease or illness that is related to sorrow or anxiety. Furthermore, the jet is a protector and energetic purifier that can keep unproductive, pessimistic, or generally negative energies (and entities) at bay.

K

Kunzite

This crystal allows the heart chakra to accept healing that it thinks it doesn't deserve, and the healing it enacts tends to reverberate out onto one's community without too much effort on the individual's part. It calms the over-excitable nervous system, too.

Kyanite

This "bladed" crystal has the potential to align all the chakras. It boosts energy by removing blockages and strengthening intuition. Through its use, one's speech and thoughts will become more and more aligned with one's deeper sense of truth.

Black Kyanite, the stone of revitalization, clears blockages, stimulates energetic awakening, and helps one ground during the process.

Blue Kyanite helps its holder or wearer receive psychic messages and unlock psychic gifts.

L

Labradorite

As one of the most impressively beautiful crystals in existence (in my opinion), labradorite is also packed with healing potential. It connects one with his or her soul mission, helps the individual see the light in dark times, encourages patience and acceptance of flaws, and inspires with its gorgeous flashes of color. It can even help release feelings of exhaustion caused by over-working and distraction.

Lapis Lazuli

This stunning stone links with the throat and third eye chakras, so it allows one to overcome psychic roadblocks as well as ones dealing with communication or self-expression. It essentially encourages the individual to speak up for what he or she believes in. Furthermore, this stone is incredibly effective in healing the nervous system, the throat, and in reversing any issues relating to metabolism.

Larimar

Larimar is an incredibly useful stone that helps those seeking inspiration or understanding. It also links with the throat, third eye, and crown chakras, encouraging awakening and enlightenment on several levels. It's a great stone for diagnosing places in your body that hold disease (even if you're not consciously aware of it yet).

Lepidolite

This purple crystal helps those in need of immediate transition. Whether you're moving, changing jobs, switching gears in life, or otherwise, lepidolite will be your best aid in those highly changeable (and often frustrating) moments. Furthermore, lepidolite reduces stress and opens one up to senses of universal awareness far greater than he or she is alone. It also can locate places that hold disease in the body, just like larimar.

Lodestone

Naturally, magnetic lodestone provides a visual aid for what it does. Just like it can draw iron shavings its way, it pulls in abundance from all corners of the world just for its holder and that person's community. Associated with luck, endurance, growth, and relief from pain, confusion, or burden, lodestone has a lot to provide. It can even help one establish balance and help heal the blood or broken bones.

M

Magnesite

Magnesite is a great meditation aid. It also boosts unconditional love of others, and it provides a general sense of calm for its wearer or holder. It brings about an overall feeling of harmony for anyone around it. Physically, magnesite is also high in magnesium, which allows it to heal muscle pains and aches, encourage muscle growth, and reduce the frequency of cramps. This stone also brings down fever effectively, eliminating one's sickness, and its related irritabilities.

Magnetite

Like lodestone, magnetite is naturally magnetic, but it works less through drawing in abundance than lodestone does. Instead, magnetite pulls together and eliminates toxicity, physically, energetically, and aurally. It can provide the opposite energy level that you're currently experiencing through its magnetic capacities, too. If you're an asthmatic or someone who has frequent nosebleeds, magnetite will also be incredibly helpful to ease your physical symptoms.

Malachite

This powerful energetic amplifier works well against arthritis and other joint pains/issues. For friendships, it enhances feelings of love and trust. For healing, it eliminates stress and helps the heart. For well-being, it clears the heart chakra and paves the way for productive transformation.

Moldavite

Moldavite is a fragment of meteorite, so its abilities are fairly unique. This dark green stone aids spiritual development, increases receptivity to visions and sparks important life changes. It also relates to the circulation system through its connection to the heart chakra (as well as to the optical system through the third eye chakra and the nervous system through the crown chakra).

Moonstone

Moonstone is highly connected with feminine universal energy, women, and the literal moon of Earth. It can help one become more accepting of their cycles and fluctuations, however, even if they're not female or overly feminine. Essentially, this stone boosts your psychic powers and protects your energy.

Black Moonstone is a little more complex than standard moonstone, for it relates to the energy of the Black Madonna, Lilith, Kali, Hekate, and more. Instead of focusing on the bright, illuminating powers of the moon, this stone looks at the power of remaining hidden and what shadow really is (spoiler alert: it's not evil, it's just an energetic compliment to light).

Morganite

This stone helps one process trauma by cleansing the heart chakra of its lingering wounds, and it also helps encourage emotional growth toward wisdom. It reminds its holder or wearer that we are all vessels of and channels for divine love. For those with anxiety or stress disorders, morganite will be a godsend. For those goals of astral travel and healing, morganite will be your closest ally.

Muscovite

Muscovite is a form of naturally-occurring mica. It helps one connect to his or her higher self to receive guidance or healing, and it encourages transformation on all levels. For those with kidney, sleep, or allergy problems, muscovite might do just the trick! For those with anxiety and stress issues, too, this crystal is a keeper.

N

Natrolite

This crystal is a highly energetic form of zeolite, and it works well to heal vision or brain disorders because it also connects with the third eye and crown chakras. If you seek guidance in your healing from ascended masters, your higher self, your ancestors, or higher dimensional beings, natrolite can help you make and maintain contact to suit that goal.

Nebula Stone

Nebula stone enacts its best healing potential on the cellular level. If you want to kickstart autophagy or fight a degenerative disorder, this stone will be a go-to for you. Similarly, if you're healing from any major injury, a nebula stone by your side *could* work miracles.

Nuummite

This black stone works well to maintain a healthy balance of blood sugar, as it naturally purifies the blood of its holder or wearer. If you have troubles with pain or sleep, nuummite is good to have handy, for it neutralizes pain and helps to induce periods of insightful and deep rest. It can also help one feel empowered to face his or her fears and grow beyond them.

O

Obsidian

Generally, obsidian protects its holder and absorbs negative energy, whether emotionally, electromagnetically, or otherwise. Obsidian is a good stone for people who struggle with depression, too, because it allows one to see the bright side of things and relax enough to enjoy what's happening. Furthermore, all obsidians are skilled at revitalization and resolution. Finally, if you're still trying to figure out what exactly to heal within you, obsidian can help pinpoint the source of your disease.

Apache Tear can help resolve ancestral and past live traumas or wounds. It is also attuned to heal in times of incredible distress in the present. In general, it's a good detoxifying stone, too.

Rainbow Obsidian has somewhat of a gentler energy than harsher, completely black obsidian. For those in need of help with grounding or with healing one's connection to the earth, this type of obsidian will be perfect.

Snowflake Obsidian has a great tie to ancestral healing, and it resonates with the sacral chakra. Its effect is soothing and centering. For help with circulation and skeletal strength, this stone is a go-to.

Onyx

Onyx is a very supportive stone. Whatever you're going through, onyx can make the situation seem easier or more approachable or manageable. It builds confidence and focuses one's attention. Like other black stones, it can help resolve feelings of grief or sadness, too. For physical healing, onyx has an affinity for the bones, teeth, and feet.

Opal

This brilliant mostly white stone has the ability to awaken your true potential, whether magically, intellectually, athletically, or otherwise. It helps its holder or wearer stay calm but focused on his or her current mission. It connects with the dream world and healthy sleep, and it can reduce or eliminate infections, fevers, and all-consuming anger.

Black-Brown-Gray Opal, in particular, heals one's reproductive system and can help the individual separate sexual compulsions from their emotional origins, allowing him or her to heal the emotional problem first before lashing out sexually.

Blue Opal builds and boosts confidence through demeanor and speech. It has a calming energy, too, that helps the holder or wearer stay connected to his or her higher self despite struggles or stress.

Cherry Opal can help dissolve headaches, muscle pains, and menopausal struggles. It's great for blood and tissue healing as well.

Chrysopal is blue-green in color, and it has an effect on its holder or wearer that he or she is looking through rose-colored glasses at the world. It's a liver detoxifier, too, and it works wonders for chest congestion.

Fire Opal gives warning signs against danger as it protects its holder or wearer. It rejuvenates one's passion and fire for life, and it helps those who work against injustice. For the physical body, fire opal has an affinity for the kidneys, adrenals, reproductive organs, and intestines.

Green Opal helps one recover from toxic or painful relationships by adjusting the mind to handle what happened, learn from it, and grow. It boosts the immune system, too, and works like a champ against any flu or cold symptoms.

Hyalite is a water opal that connects with spiritual worlds, both alongside and far removed from our own. Use during meditation or astral traveling for grounding and connectivity with the divine.

P

Peridot

Peridot helps lonely people make friends, and then it can also help people who have troubles with jealousy or anger be more rational to keep the friends they have. It links to the heart chakra but heals wounds on mind, body, and soul levels.

Petalite

This crystal is said to connect its holder to the angels or highest dimensional realms and consciousnesses. For those who aren't quite there yet, it can awaken shamanic capacities, help one find their path, allow one to trigger their soul mission, and activate huge growth patterns. Physically, petalite can help those suffering from AIDS and cancer through its cellular, intestinal, respiratory, and muscular benefits.

Prehnite

This green stone connects with the heart chakra and allows its holder or wearer to experience and reflect outwards unconditional love. It's protective and motivating. In terms of helping others find peace, it can work particularly well for hoarders, hyperactive individuals and kids, bipolar individuals, and those out of touch with nature.

Pyrite

Iron pyrite, or fool's gold, is a powerful stone for people with hormonal imbalances. In addition, people who are teased for being feminine or masculine when they "shouldn't" be will find comfort through this stone, and it is a great companion for anyone transitioning physically in terms of sex or socially in terms of gender identity. It also protects its wearer or holder from environmental and electromagnetic pollutants. Finally, it aids in boosting willpower, immunity, and cardiovascular health.

Pyrolusite

This shiny, fanlike mineral helps transform disease into future strength, manipulation into communication, and expectations into acceptance. Generally, it's a motivator of transformation on all levels, but only when the transformation suits one's overall health, growth, soul mission, and overall potential. For the physical body, pyrolusite aids with metabolism regulation, bronchitis & eyesight treatments, and circulation strengthening.

Q

Quartz

While there are tens if not hundreds of different types of quartz, they all work incredibly well with the healing of many natures. Regardless of what part of the body you're working on or what aspect of personality, quartz can help you discern what needs fixing and what to do about it. Then, quartz can store and amplify energies in order to go about the healing you desire. It's great for any chakra and any ailment or situation.

R

Rhodochrosite

This pink and white stone has an affinity for love and the heart chakra. It helps one connect to and love the earth as well, especially if the individual has already conquered the self-love bit. For those experiencing personality deficit or mid-life crisis, rhodochrosite can help you remember and reconnect to who you truly are.

Physically, rhodochrosite heals the lungs and eases breathing-related problems.

Rhodonite

Rhodonite helps even the lowliest hermit connect to the sense of brotherly love that inspires all of humanity. It's great for anti-social individuals in that sense. In addition, it helps people healing PTSD through its affinity for those in the fight, flight, or freeze modes. Whether you're feeling shock, paralysis, panic, or fear, rhodonite can help you move past that and remember how to be yourself again or how to become the *new you*. Physically, it heals insect bites, reduces the presence of scars, fights inflammation on a number of levels (including ulcers!), and eases autoimmune diseases.

Rhyolite

This more-rare stone inspires deep and moving creativity without forcing its flow. It connects to deep meditation states and heals past life wounds with ease. Rhyolite has an emotional balancing effect that encourages strength and self-esteem even against the most challenging emotional ordeals. Physically, rhyolite can be used to mitigate infections and assimilate vitamin B. It's good for body-builders or those working on strength training, too, due to its ability to increase both strength and muscle tone.

Rose Quartz

Rose quartz is a crystal intimately tied up in ideas of love. It attracts love, but only the love we think we deserve, for it teaches the holder or wearer that one cannot "deserve" a love that one cannot afford oneself. It works for circulatory system healing and relieves symptoms of emotional or physical traumas. Use this crystal for any healing work dealing with self-esteem, personality, love, forgiveness, or the literal and physical heart.

Ruby

Ruby, whether in gemstone form or simply polished or uncut, is a powerful motivator, connector to bliss, and locator of passions. It's an incredibly dynamic stone that gives energy to whatever area of your life needs it. Whether you need help with becoming a better leader, healing the blood, fighting infection, stimulating overall health, expressing emotionally, or what have you, ruby will help you concentrate and achieve your goals.

S

Sapphire

This stone comes in a variety of colors and forms, but it always helps enact genuine and creative self-expression. Sapphire also builds a sense of deep inner peace and attracts romantic love when desired. It works specifically well to heal the eyes, the glands, and the veins. It's commonly called the wisdom stone, too, with its intrinsic links to the third eye and throat chakras.

Sardonyx

Sardonyx is good for regulating, strength-building, endurance-boosting, and protecting. It encourages happiness and good luck as well as self-control and stamina. In terms of the physical body, sardonyx helps one absorb all the nutrients of one's food, and it encourages the waste elimination process to work well. Furthermore, works incredibly well for skeletal and respiratory healing.

Selenite

Selenite crystals are powerful cleansers and chargers. When you're looking for a way to cleanse your crystals, look to selenite first! Get a selenite slab or block to make things easy on yourself. This crystal absorbs and transmutes all negative energy into that which your higher self can work with. It connects with past life healing, too. Physically, selenite strengthens the spine, removes toxic metals from the blood, encourages healthy breastfeeding, and protects against epileptic seizures.

Serpentine

Serpentine clears all the chakras and helps the crown chakra open to receive information and teachings from the higher self. It helps one feel more in control of his or her life, and it eliminates parasites of all natures. Figuratively, serpentine removes psychic vampires and energetic parasites from your path. Literally, serpentine cleanse your gut and body of parasites that harm your abilities to absorb nutrients and build strong bones. This stone also works well for diabetics.

Smoky Quartz

This crystal is a version of clear brown quartz that has the special capacity to remove negative energies from your path. Whether they arrive in the form of electromagnetic radiation or pollutants, negative emotions from others, or bad habits of your own, these negative energies will have no choice but to be eradicated in the presence of smoky quartz. If you struggle with removing these shadows from your life even with smoky quartz, try boosting your willpower and strengthening the solar plexus chakra, too. Use a piece of gold or yellow quartz along with your smoky quartz and see what happens.

Sodalite

Sodalite is a great stone for group work, as it encourages feelings of friendship, trust, companionship, and solidarity for the task at hand. It also helps you stay true to yourself despite any adversaries, and for those who struggle with defensiveness or defensive personality traits, sodalite can help melt your harsh exterior and pave the way for growth.

Stichtite

This purple stone has a powerful connection to the third eye and the heart chakras. If you're feeling emotional distress of any nature, stichtite will be there to comfort you. If you're having issues with digestion, stichtite may help you realize how your problems have an emotional root (as well as what steps to take to fix the situation). If you feel alone and lost without anyone to help you, stichtite's rescuing nature will be activated too, calling to you people who will be able to help. It's a powerful healing stone for many emotional imbalances.

Sugilite

Sugilite is a stone oriented to boost love. It helps you love yourself and understand why you chose this life for this current incarnation. It also helps you love others and practice forgiveness in any format. It helps one understand the connection between mind and body, too, and that understanding is pivotal in the healing of overall disease. For help with headaches, restless limbs, and general discomfort, sugilite is a great choice. Hold next to the body part that hurts to receive the greatest relief.

Sunstone

Sunstone helps fight depression by turning sorrow into lasting happiness and bliss for life. It helps you remember how to nurture yourself in times of need, and it can also attract nurturing help if you're unable to get there yourself. If you're feeling drained or exhausted, sunstone can pick you up and give you the energy you need. If you're feeling low and pessimistic, sunstone can get you back to seeing the glass as half full. For the physical body, sunstone removes ulcers, relieves sore throats, kickstarts the immune system, and reminds you of your abilities to heal yourself from the start.

T

Tanzanite

This crystal works amazingly well for skin and vision issues. Figuratively, too, it helps you achieve the foresight you need to attain your goals, and it allows you the ability to receive psychic visions through meditation. It connects to the crown, third eye, and throat chakras, too, bringing voice to the body itself.

Tektite

This extraterrestrial stone helps one communicate with other worlds. It balances energy flow in the body and clears the chakras, sometimes fully opening them on contact (as with the third eye chakra). Physically, tektite is a good companion for anyone seeking a fertility boost, and it can reduce the intensity of any fever. After surgery, tektite is beneficial to have around to stimulate easy, quick healing.

Tiger's Eye

Tiger's eye has a lucky, abundant vibe that wants to attract wealth and success into your life. It connects with the solar plexus chakra to bring feelings of confidence, willpower, positivity, and true joy. If you're dealing with feelings of unworthiness, tiger's eye is a must-have. Physically, tiger's eye links with the eyes and helps repair broken bones.

Blue Tiger's Eye calms down one's energy. If you're overactive in terms of sex, metabolism, anger, or fears, this stone will help you reground and re-center yourself in relation to those intense stresses and their true emotional causes.

Hawk's Eye is a particular pattern within the tiger's eye banding that looks like the eye of a hawk, and it helps with literal vision healing as well as figurative third-eye healing through divination capabilities, insight and intuition, and psychic abilities like clairvoyance and clairaudience.

Red Tiger's Eye boosts one's energy. If you're feeling lazy, unproductive, stagnant, lost, or lethargic, this stone can help you find your drive and motivation once more.

Topaz

Topaz of any color encourages openness, trust, and friendship through increased understanding and patience. It encourages one to feel generous and fortunate in all situations. That self-realization is key to one's ability to attract future abundance with this stone as well. Physically, this crystal links with regenerative tissue capacities.

Imperial Topaz reminds one of the highest possible good and helps one align his or her work with this potential. Furthermore, it strengthens manifestation abilities and enforces transformative success.

Tourmaline

Tourmaline fights stagnation of any kind. It encourages action and fights fatigue. If fatigue is triggered by anemia, tourmaline goes straight to the source and works to heal the imbalance. It also connects with overall energies of attracting success and love into its holder's (or wearer's) life.

Black Tourmaline works for grounding and balancing the individual. It also redirects negativity send your way, and it can remind you of the benefits of reasonable control and discipline.

Pink Tourmaline is also known as rubellite, and it heals the heart both physically and figuratively. Its soothing and insightful energy is particularly helpful for break-ups or loss.

Watermelon Tourmaline works well for people who are easily overwhelmed or highly sensitive. It can help you maintain perspective in any situation, no matter how difficult. It also activates the heart chakra and works to purify the blood.

Turquoise

Turquoise is a good meditation aid for any situation, as it relaxes and purifies the mind. It also helps one channel kindness constantly by detoxifying the aura when interacting with other people. Furthermore, it detoxifies the body and works to fight inflammation in a variety of ways. It also builds tissue, helps nutrient absorption, and defeats infection with ease.

U

Ulexite

Ulexite is a crystal also known as TV stone, and it's called that for its incredible clarity and ability to magnify what's seen through it. It helps to cleanse problem routines and activate healthier ones, and it allows you to see your hopes manifested in the physical world. Physically, it heals the eyes and can fight aging in the skin.

Unakite

This green and pink stone have great reproductive healing potential as well as the potential for psychic awakening. When you combine those two purposes of the stone, it becomes clear how the stone could encourage the *rebirthing* of yourself into higher levels of your potential! Physically, unakite boosts recovery in any situation and maintains hair and tissue growth. Furthermore, it does several things to make sure you have the most healthy pregnancy possible, such as maintain proper body weight, cleanse the reproductive system, and align mama's system with baby's as best as possible.

V

Vanadinite

This crystal works well to heal bladder and prostate problems in men that cause excessive urination. For people of all genders, vanadinite assists comfort on earth and abilities to travel to other dimensions. Furthermore, it gives a boost in meditation through its abilities to cut off excess mental chatter when you attempt to concentrate on the moment and your breath.

Variscite

Variscite reminds of the importance of hope. For people with terminal or chronic conditions – or people who are home-bound / house-bound or differently-abled – this crystal keeps the spirits up and the goals focused. It relaxes the troubled mind and makes sure one's dreams for healing are realistic but not fatalistic. Physically, it encourages elasticity of skin and plasticity of the brain. It even neutralizes problematic acidic conditions in the body that can lead to cancer.

Vesuvianite

This crystal is also sometimes called idocrase, and it generally aids with self-awareness and self-restraint, especially for those triggered by thoughts (or memories) of literal imprisonment or restraint. Furthermore, this stone encourages desires for freedom and connects the individual with outlets for his or her creativity. For those struggling with fear, it will release you. For those hungry to learn, it will direct you.

W

Wavellite

This mineral is known to balance one's energy flow, whether it's the flow of blood, breath, emotions, or life energy (also called *prana* or *chi*). It brings awareness to the individual of this energy flow, too, reminding them of the law of One and the importance of peace and love in the universe. For skin conditions and abusive living situations, wavellite helps the individual finally find some relief.

Wulfenite

This crystal helps one accept and transmute negativity in certain situations to positivity if the individual starts to get depressed about things. Furthermore, if you've had trouble sugarcoating things and looking too much on the bright side unrealistically, wulfenite can remind of the importance of hardship and strife. It's a grounding stone that connects knowledge and pain directly to wisdom and growth. Physically, it builds or conserves your energy, when needed.

Z

Zebra Stone

Zebra stone stimulates energy and ends stagnant cycles. It also affirms strength, endurance, and stamina. In that sense, this stone is a great companion for athletes and competitive runners. Furthermore, it is wonderful for anyone who struggles with procrastination for any type of work. Physically, zebra stone has an affinity for skeletal healing with particular focuses on the spine and on the bones of older individuals. For people dealing with heart murmurs, heart spasms, or muscle tremors, zebra stone is equally helpful.

Zeolite

This type of crystal is actually a generic name for any group of crystals growing in a cluster on a matrix of standard rock or standard quartz. The combination of the crystal points in the cluster magnifies the energy of the piece and focuses it on tasks like detoxifying, aligning energies, igniting awareness, building strength, encouraging fertility, or anything else you decide as your goal. Physically, zeolite clusters work well to treat goiters and eliminate addictions (and their underlying emotional causes).

Zincite

Zincite is able to stimulate, align, and cleanse all the chakras while providing an energy boost to the rest of your system, too. It's especially powerful when it comes to rebuilding one's passion and fire for life, and it links well with courageous goals. In terms of the physical body, zincite heals both the hair and the skin, and for men, its effects on the prostate are unmatched, while for women, its assistance during menopause is a blessing.

Zircon

Sometimes we judge ourselves far harsher than anyone else would dare. Even if we don't realize we're falling into that pattern of action, zircon can snap anyone out of it. It awakens self-awareness and shuts down bad habits and routines. As it cuts out the "should" and "have to" energy of your self-judgment, zircon enables you to meet and validate your *true* and most authentic self. In that sense, it encourages transformative growth.

Zoisite

Zoisite protects against electromagnetic radiations that are problematic for the human body, so keep a piece on your laptop or next to your phone when it's charging! It also encourages feelings of appreciation, vitality, and divine love (even in the face of despair and rejection). It can also help you become aware of your defense mechanisms and restructure them to be healthier and more productive. Physically, zoisite is a detoxifier that stimulates health of the reproductive, cellular, circulatory, endocrine, and immune systems.

What Forms of Crystals Do What?

Particularly when it comes to grid work with crystals, simply knowing which one is which and sensing where to put it may not be enough. The added layer to complete your work will be learning what *forms* of crystals do what. It could be that a pointed crystal completes your grid in a way that a polished version of the same specimen cannot.

It could also be that your grids are equally powerful regardless of what form of the crystal you use. It partially depends on your mindset and partially depends on your abilities, financially, spiritually, and otherwise. Regardless of your current means, however, the knowledge is always helpful, I say! When you *are* able to, the following details will become applicable, but for now, take in what you can and intuit the rest as you're able.

Polished

All polished or "tumbled" stones are considered basically **egg-shaped crystals**, and they carry with them an intrinsically balancing, comforting energy, especially when they're larger polished stones.

These egg-shaped crystals can be large enough to fit in your palm, and then they're called **palm stones**, and they're usually flat on one side and rounded otherwise. These varieties are more grounding than simply balancing, and they'll also work well as reflexology or massage tools.

Sometimes, you'll find these tumbled stones in the true **sphere, or ball format**. The beauty of these balls is that it looks smooth and perfect on the outside, but if the crystal is even semi-translucent, you can see the imperfections, flaws, and separate planes inside that space which makes the ball a more complex healing medium. It can amplify energies in ways a flattened side cannot, and it's said that these ball shapes can even be used as so-called "windows" into time, space, or other worlds.

Generally, polished stones hold a more harnessed and compact energy and vibration than, say, a raw mineral or a pointed crystal would. These "tumbled" stones have likely spent hours in a rock tumbler to become that way, which both shocks the stone and *affirms* its vibration, again and again, honing and perfecting its own energetic intention. Therefore, if you only have tumbled stones to work with, fear not! You've got a powerful set of minerals and crystals at your disposal, to be sure, and their form affirms that completely.

Raw & Geodes

Tumbled and polished stones and gems, of course, have to start somewhere! There is a gorgeous raw format of each mineral and crystal, whether it's a small and perfect ruby gemstone in a matrix of clear quartz or a giant slab of selenite. When it comes to the details of those raw versions, there are a few things to keep in mind.

First, consider the **cluster of crystals**. The cluster naturally has several pointed ends coming from the same surface or base. Those points may all go out in various directions or they all may point the same way, but the general effect in healing and gridding is the same. Because there are so many of the same type growing out of the same base, clusters, therefore, expel their energy and healing vibration out exponentially more efficiently than a single point would. The energy of a cluster can fill a room or even a home without much effort on its holder's part.

Second, consider the **geode**! Geodes are essentially a world of crystals contained within what looks like a rock. When you crack the rock open, you see that it's been completely lined on the inside with the crystal you desire. In this format, therefore, the crystals' vibrations exude a gentler and less direct force on their surroundings. Think about it, the crystals are homed in this cave-like vessel, and their points will all face one another; that inward-faced energy sends out slow and steady vibrational assistance to the geode's surroundings, depending on how big the geode cluster is (in both size and number). Geodes have a guardian-like presence in healing, too, and work particularly well to break bad habits and reprogram addictions.

Third, consider the **naturally-occurring square** (also called "cube") or **triangle** (also called "pyramid") crystalline structures. Some minerals that naturally grow into square shapes are fluorite and iron pyrite, while the most common triangular ones are often apophyllite. Essentially, squares are excellent for grounding and intentional work, for they keep their energy locked inside their forms. They offer a more concentrated, focused healing effort than, say, a cluster or a geode. They're good to keep in your pocket throughout the day or to use in the center of a grid.

On the other hand, triangles are often human-made by cutting off a single-pointed crystal right at the base of the point, but even when they're human-made, the effect is generally the same. These pyramid formations magnify the energy of your intention and focus it through the top point, honing your intention and fully concentrating your healing efforts. Triangle formations are powerful aids in chakra healing as well because they can draw out negativity or blockages from your chakras, transmuting all that into positivity then releasing it all out and through their pyramids' tips. (Clearly, as mentioned before, the naturally-occurring triangle formation is more ideal than the human-altered one, but you should take what you can get!)

And fourth, consider the generally **amorphous raw mineral**. Without any inherent structure aside from being unpolished, these minerals and crystals have a fiercer, relatively less structured effect in their healing compared to the cube, pyramid, or even the geode. It happens that their vibrations are stalwartly expressed in the instant with direct effect toward your intention. Raw and formless minerals like this are great centerpieces for grids, as the surrounding assembly of crystals can help to focus and sustain the amorphous vibration for more intensive healing work.

Finally, your raw crystals can be pointed on one or both ends, causing them to have facets, and that's a whole other ballgame, which we'll venture into momentarily. For now, know that the four main raw forms of crystals and minerals affect their energies and expressions in terms of healing. However, if all you have happens to be an amorphous tiger's eye, don't go out and replace it with a polished one just because!

There's no reason to rush or overspend when working with crystal healing. Just remember to trust in the Goddess, your guides, the universe, God, truth, or whatever you call that energy that's bigger than us. Trust in that energy, and trust that all the tools you believe you need for healing will come to you in time.

Faceted

Faceted crystals are described in these terms to express the multi-sided nature of that raw crystal. Within the category of faceted crystals, there are several different forms to work with, four of which we'll walk through today. First, there's the generally **single-pointed crystal**. Maybe it grew out of a matrix of another stone or maybe it broke off of a cluster of its buddies. Regardless, this crystal has one side that's dull and one side that's naturally pointed.

This first type of crystal would have the ability to harness energy toward the direction of the mineral's tip. Essentially, that single point works incredibly well for healing, because it allows the healer to extract pure energy from him or herself and send it into the patient purified with the vibration of the crystal – or because it allows the individual to draw out what's impure from him or herself and direct it away by pointing the tip elsewhere and expelling it from the crystal afterward.

Second, the crystal could be naturally double-ended in points, and then it would be called "**double-terminated**." Crystals like Herkimer diamond are naturally double-terminated, so they (and others like them) are able to release or absorb energy equally well out of each side. These crystals and minerals would be able to move energy *through* them in one direction like pointed crystals, but their special form would enable them to move energy in *two* directions at once, making a (potentially) more balanced approach to energetic healing.

Third, the crystal could be **tabular**, which is when it's almost a flat sheet with single- or double-pointed ends. Instead of having anywhere from three to ten facets on the sides, therefore, it would really just have two well-defined, broadsides. These types of crystals and minerals likely have notches and raw exposures connecting those two well-defined sides, and there's extra potential in healing if you have these crystals to rub those side notches. This gesture will activate and focus the crystal's energy and any healing guidance it might contain for you.

Fourth and finally, the crystal could be a **long point** that just formed itself that way. This version is similar to a double-terminated crystal, but it's usually much longer and thinner. These thin wand-like growths of crystals have similar energy to what they resemble. If you're hoping to focus the crystal's energy, hold the formation like a wand and direct its vibration. These types of formations are applicable for ritual work and deep cleansing work of any healing inclination.

Harvested Yourself

Raw minerals and crystals can be found anywhere on Earth. Sometimes, they can even be found in your own backyard! You'd be surprised what minerals and crystals comprise the bedrock of your town and then end up scattered in its surrounding soils.

That being said, you can choose to sift through your soil and see what's there (often just a bit of mica and plenty of quartz, but it always depends!), or you can go crystal hunting! Based on where you are in the world, your range of options may be incredibly limited or bountiful. You may have to drive hours to days, or you may have to drive 5 minutes away.

Look into it! Do the research and see where your favorite minerals and crystals are found in real time. If you can go there, go there! Guaranteed, there are mines you can go to or places you can hike to that grant you the opportunity to extract minerals for yourself, and that experience compares to none other.

True, you might not have all the tools you need but you can surely pick up a few!

True, you might not be that skilled with the area when you arrive at the location, but you can always make friends with someone from the community and figure out the lay of the land!

True, you might not get those "perfect" specimens that get sold online for small fortunes. However, the experience of going out yourself and connecting to the earth and its blessings (these beautiful nature bits), your relationship with the mineral will be completely different, and its vibration will be all the more attuned to you, your goals, and your healing intentions.

Imported

The complete reverse of the minerals you harvest yourself is those that come imported from the opposite side of the planet. Surely, these stones are powerful and vibrationally energetic, just like you need them to be. There's nothing inherently *wrong* with these imported specimens, but there is one main thing to be conscious of when you *do* pick up crystals of this nature.

Consider *where* the stone came from. If you have the ability to know what country or continent it came from, do a little research. What is the quality of life like? How do most people make their living? Are peoples' lives in this area tied to a mineral economy in that location? Could it be that your purchase subtly influences a problematic regime?

The more conscious you are about your purchases, the more enlightened your healing will become. If it happens to be that you're using an imported crystal from a strife-torn area, cleanse it a little extra before you use it on yourself, and when you *do* use it, send a little love to the miner and country of origin!

If you have more than one of this type of stone, devote a little extra love to them. You could try cleansing them all together (see chapter 2 for some cleansing tips and instructions!) and sending some healing vibrations out into the world for the people who mined them from the earth. Respect toward this origin space, environmentally and culturally, in your healing work will help both *it* and *you* evolve.

CHAPTER 4
Explaining Chakra Healing

A lot of the crystal listings of the previous chapter kept mentioning a particular (and potentially unfamiliar) word again and again. I wonder if you noticed it? "Chakra." The listings read that this crystal opens that chakra. This mineral clears all the chakras, and more as the list goes on.

While some of you will already know what this word means, others may not. Even if you do know, there's always more to learn! And what's more, it can't help to be reminded of the incredible healing capacity you hold when you combine crystal healing with chakra healing.

What Are the Chakras? What Is the Kundalini?

"Chakra" is another word for the wheel in Sanskrit, a language that originated from ancient India almost 4,000 years ago. While chakra literally translates to the wheel, however, it more so means an energetic wheel that churns and spins, pushing life force energy through anything with life. As humans, we have 7 chakras housed in our physical bodies, and these energy wheels connect to 7 main glands in the lymphatic system across our bodies.

While the chakras connect to glands, they also correlate with specific things, experiences, and emotions as well as particular colors. The first chakra called the Root Chakra or "Muladhara" is located in the genitals, and it relates to the color red, affecting one's senses of safety, security, well-being, survival, and sexuality. The second chakra called the Sacral Chakra or "Svadhishthana" is located below the belly button, and it relates to the color orange, affecting one's capacities of pleasure, belongingness, community, creativity, and emotionality. The third chakra called the Solar Plexus Chakra or "Manipura" is located on the diaphragm, and it relates to the color yellow, affecting one's will-power, the force of desire, assertiveness, need for control, and confidence.

The fourth chakra called the Heart Chakra or "Anahata" is located at the heart, and it relates to the color green, affecting one's abilities to feel love, compassion, relatability, understanding, warmth, and joy. The fifth chakra called the Throat Chakra or "Vishuddha" is located in the throat and neck, and it relates to the color blue, affecting one's capacities of speech, self-expression, group communication, listening, and purpose-finding. The sixth chakra called the Third Eye Chakra or "Anja" is located between one's eyebrows, and it relates to the color indigo, affecting one's powers of foresight, intuition, self-awareness, psychism, and higher consciousness. Finally, the seventh chakra called the Crown Chakra or "Sahasrara" is located at the top point of the skull, and it relates to the color violet, affecting one's connection to the divine, spirituality, the Universe, the Earth, and more.

In chapter 5, we'll go on to discuss how particular colors have vibrations oriented to heal in different ways, but for now, it will suffice to say that these chakras and their respective colors made links with certain energetic expressions of the individual. If one's chakras are imbalanced in any way by being blocked, spinning backward, spinning too slow, or spinning too fast, chakra *healing* would come into the mix.

Chakra healing focuses on the flow of these energy wheels in the body, the health of their respective glands, and their effect on the overall person. Chakra healing aims to open, cleanse, and align all the chakras so that energy flows as freely and limitlessly as possible, allowing for the kundalini to rise.

"Kundalini" is another Indian Sanskrit term, and this one means small, coiled one. What it refers to is what the language calls a serpent lying coiled and dormant at the base of one's spine until awakened and invited to dance through the free-flowing chakra wheels, providing healing to the individual's entire body and spirit.

What Is a Kundalini Awakening?

When the kundalini becomes awakened, that small, coiled one becomes larger and vibrant with life. During this period, the chakras must have already been cleared, opened, and aligned or balanced to a certain degree so that at least all are open-ish and flowing in the right direction. With this relative free-flow of inner subtle energies, the serpent at the base of one's spine gets excited and begins its track of movement.

It may sound like this all happens very quickly, but it's exactly the opposite. It can take months to years to be able to heal, cleanse, and open a stubborn or traumatized chakra, and even then, it could be that your other chakras become blocked because of such long-standing focus on just one. That being said, simply balancing one's chakras can take a good bit of time, but once they're becoming open and balanced, that serpent can't help but become engaged.

The kundalini symbolizes one's connection to the divine. It is that divine energy (like "prana," "chi," or even "reiki") of the universe that inspires the kundalini's movement when the chakras work with a balanced flow. That divine energy is termed Shakti in this tradition of study and healing, but the gist is quite clear; once one's body is open enough for the spirit to move freely, his or her connection to the divine will be boosted, bringing the individual to an enlightened, awakened energetic state.

As you progress through your own kundalini awakening, meditation will be your best and most supportive friend. Through conscious and mindful meditation, you'll become able to guide the snake's movement through your chakras, feeling its flow bringing enlightenment and insight to your various energy centers. You'll be able to slow down your attention and focus, drowning out the stresses of the day in order to focus on the healing going on inside of you, for the movement of the kundalini reverberates its own type of a cure out from the inside out with each turn of its tail.

Once your kundalini becomes awakened through conscious attention, mindfulness, visualization, or otherwise, some things you might experience are as follows, and during the first stages of one's kundalini awakening, things will not be easy, for the energetic healing of the kundalini will make things uncomfortable at first. You might get literally stinky. You might get moody. You might have an emotional outburst. You might feel uncomfortable in your own skin but stick through it! Some things need to be cleansed out in order for growth to be made!

Once you get through that harsh first set of steps, you'll experience more positive effects, such as clearer sense of life direction, connection to soul purpose, confidence in one's self and purpose, awareness of one's true potential, heightened senses, increased joy and openness, budding or bursting creativity, and manifestation capabilities.

However, alongside all this positive, hopeful news, one thing must be kept in mind: the kundalini cannot (and will not) be awakened with self-serving thoughts. The trick to this process is to act and meditate selflessly, allowing the ego to become muted and one's connection to pure universal energy to flourish. Focusing on the end-goal will not work, for it's all about the process and what's taught (and learned) along the way.

How Is Crystal Healing Connected with the Chakras?

Crystal healing and chakra healing have an intimate and intrinsic connection. Chakra healing spends its remedial attention on the flow of our internal energies. These energies are physical, sure, relating to specific parts of the body, self-expression, organs, glands, lymphatic systems, and more, but they're also so much more than just physical.

Sometimes, studying the patterns of the physical itself can also teach us a lot about how energy works and flows, and these studies are based in what's called the *meta*physical. Metaphysically, energy, blood, vibrations, fluids, and more all want to *flow*, and blockages in that flow happen. However, they don't always happen due to these directly-physical causes. Instead, sometimes looking closer at things, at the metaphysical details, can be all the help one needs.

In the process of chakra healing, blockages and flow are central. They're studied to figure out what needs to be fixed and what's working, as well as what needs just a little boost or adjustment to flow correctly. When you meet a blockage head-on, however, the cause of the blockage will likely still be unclear, and then those metaphysical clues are one's greatest help. When you think about the blockage there, what comes to mind? With a heart blockage, for instance, what associations surface? What causes can you intuit, and what symptoms would you expect from this malady, based on the patterns of those physical behaviors?

Once you can intuit these metaphysical connections, you'll be in a good place to add crystals to the mix. On one hand, your metaphysical associations will enable you to intuitively choose crystals, stones, and minerals that you think will work well for your healing. On the other hand, all chakras already have a color and theme associated with them, making them all the more inclined to mesh well with the metaphysical healing capacities of stones of that same color.

Whether your mixture of crystal and chakra healing focuses on this color association or the more specific healing abilities of individual stones, in particular, the energetic vibrations of each realm of healing work well when combined together. Stones can help bring awareness to issues or successes with that internal and emotional free-flow, and they can also help point out charkas that you may not realize are spinning the exact opposite direction as they should be.

Essentially, crystal healing can work like a metaphysical magnifying glass for those interested in chakra healing, and that relationship is beautiful while being mutually-beneficial, for you'll certainly learn more about each healing modality by combining them both together to meet these specific aims.

On Clearing, Aligning, and Balancing Your Chakras with Crystals

As you read before in chapter 3's index, certain crystals, minerals, gems, and stones have different metaphysical and energetic capabilities when it comes to chakra healing. Sometimes, a stone clears just one chakra, while other times one stone clears them all. Sometimes, a stone can align every chakra with one another, while other times it just works on balancing two or three in a harmony together.

Generally, what it means when it says a crystal can clear or open a chakra, this phrasing means that the crystal can pinpoint chakra blockages and work directly against that closing, destructive effort. The crystal's presence will help you process what's been holding up that chakra's flow and what it means for you personally and your day-to-day experiences. The crystal may even encourage you to see action plans for working against that blockage, but it could be that the stone just teaches you and lets you decide on *process* and *action* for yourself.

When it comes to those crystals that can align the chakras, the index refers mainly to situations where the chakras' energies might be flowing the wrong way or in noncompatible speeds. In these cases, aligners come in and help readjust the flow to be going the most productive direction, and these aligners also help to get the speed of that flow established at a rhythm that's helpful for all chakras but not too harsh on anyone. Aligners get the energy flowing the right way, but they're not always the most helpful with opening and blasting away blockages. Try pairing an aligner with an opener and see what happens! The effect may be even more powerful and impacting than what a balancer can do!

When the index says that a crystal will balance chakras, it means that it may provide some opening, clearing boosting power to your chakra healing as-is in order to get each energy wheel open and ready for business. Then, this crystal will get the energy moving in an even amount through each chakra so that the flow is established once more. Some people who approach balancers for the chakras will find that they have to do a lot of work on just one or two chakras to get this process to come to fruition – and even then, maybe only two or three found balance. Others will find that they have to work a little bit on each one and then the energy starts flowing through all seven chakras.

On another level, some people will find that their chakras blow wide open with the help of balancers, while others will feel that there are still partial blockages in each chakra that the balancer couldn't help with. In this case, it depends partially on the individual, his or her strength, and his or her degree of disease in any particular chakra, and it also depends partially on the crystal itself, for some are far more effective and naturally powerful than others, depending on the type of crystal and form.

CHAPTER 5
Other Methods Of Crystal Healing

Combining chakra healing with crystals is *literally* just the beginning.

In fact, crystal healing in and of itself is just scratching the surface of your incredible potential as an energetic being in this all-too-human existence. As you learn to trust and harness your intuition for crystal healing, you may find that you become drawn to other expressions of subtle energy as well. And what is subtle energy? Well, I'm glad you asked.

On Subtle Energy

Subtle energy exists all around us. It is released in terms of electromagnetic fields, so-called "energetic vibrations," which every carbon-based lifeforce on this planet possesses. By attuning yourself to crystal energy, as you learned how to do in chapter 2, you have started to pay closer attention to that subtle energy as it is expressed through mineral and crystal nature bits.

Subtle energy is what the ancients tapped into when they used crystals for healing and energy storage in their time. They must have been so intuitive. They were at least sensitive enough to realize that even metals, minerals, and flowers released vibrations that aligned with specific healing goals.

Subtle energy is also technically related to how chakras affect us. These "wheels" of energy that spin within us can get kicked into spinning backward or not spinning at all. The subtle energy that affects that spin comes from real-world incidents but then reverberates through you, subtly, until you find closure and/or heal yourself.

Subtle energy is expressed and affirmed through divination attempts as well. Divination almost literally means seeking into the supernatural and subtle energetic realms. In addition, any gesture encouraged by your intuition works alongside this type of vibration, and of course, subtle energy is expressed by crystals and minerals, too. That's partially what you were sensing through those experiments in chapter 2, as mentioned above.

All this means to say that crystals' subtle energy and intention affirmation finds itself amplified and directed through divination attempts, and this chapter will dive directly into that reality. We'll start off with a few more-obvious ways to amplify the subtle energy of your work, getting into direct divination-crystal correlation towards the end of this first section.

Then, we'll address five major modes of healing that lie on a spectrum, from being directly physical to predominantly energetic. As this chapter comes to a close, we'll prepare you for the future that exists outside this specific learning experience. There's only so much that can be conveyed in one book, so the final section will prepare you with an important piece of information: how to apply these crystal techniques to any mode of healing that you may run into without me as your guide.

Modalities of Crystal Healing

Crystals have so much potential. They can move and store so much information, and our abilities to learn from them are only growing. The sky's the limit, but the following section will provide details on nine specific healing capacities of crystals beyond their mere presence, which is already a lot and a blessing!

Chakra Healing

As mentioned in the previous chapter, chakra healing clearly has a space for crystal boosters. With each chakra being a different color and with them being incredibly positively affected by pyramid shapes, triangular-shaped stones of any of the 7 chakra colors are innately attuned to chakra healing work. Even if you don't have 7 pyramid stones, one of each chakra color, just one quartz or apophyllite pyramid can do the trick when used on one chakra at a time. Even more, 7 stones that aren't pyramids can work for the chakras if they're each colored after their own chakra. But of course, if you only have tumbled quartz, you can use that for each chakra instead, working one after the other or just on the one you have trouble with.

Aura Cleansing

The electromagnetic field that surrounds you has a name that you may have heard thrown around casually in spiritual circles in the past. The name is "aura," and it isn't just something people have been talking about to feel enlightened. The aura is real, and whether or not it has colors, I don't know, I don't have the gift of seeing them unlocked yet, but I do know that its presence has been verified by scientific studies and that it can be measured and healed.

As you go about aura healing, even if you can't see auras, your intuition with crystal companions will be your best guide. Without your crystals and your intuition, you might not have any direct "tap" into your aural reality, but with these things in play, you certainly will and do.

Diagnosing Sites of Disease

There are multiple crystals and minerals listed in chapter 3's Index that have specific attunements toward a diagnosis. For example, obsidian, quartz, lepidolite, and larimar are able to point out where the illness lies, and they're just four of perhaps fifty or more options. Using crystal healing to pinpoint sites of disease relies on two basic techniques.

First, you essentially use chakra healing to open, cleanse, or awaken your third eye. In this process, you'll find that your so-called "sixth sense" is ignited, and even with your eyes closed, you'll be able to intuit knowledge and receive guidance for your personal journey and healing. With this ability awakened, adding crystals that point out disease makes it a much more focused endeavor.

The second technique is meditation. Once you have your crystals and your third eye at least cleansed, come to a place of meditation where you simply focus on your breath with the intention of quieting your mind of all thoughts and emotions.

Then let your hands and the crystals do the talking. Move them over your body slowly with your energy focused into your third eye until each stone settles somewhere. It could be they all go to the same place, but it might not. This process works incredibly well for highly intuitive people.

Mitigating Illness

Through various crystal healing techniques, it is said that one can mitigate the symptoms of illness and help encourage overall wellness. Several other techniques are included in this section already, so in this segment, it should suffice to focus on remedies in the form of crystal essences.

Some stones and crystals are not suited for this type of work because you're essentially putting a stone directly in water and capturing the subtle energy of it in the liquid. Raw minerals and crystals are liable to disintegrate or lose their intricacies in water, but tumbled stones don't pose that same risk.

Therefore, to lessen the effects of certain illnesses or diseases, look up a particular crystal to find its abilities. When you have one or two that match your aims, try to make sure they're tumbled but if they're not, we have another option! Then set each one in a bowl of purified or spring water. Let the stone sit in water that's exposed to sunlight for 12 hours, if possible. If it has to be 12 hours over two or more days, that's absolutely fine.

Afterward, pour that water into a large bottle to save it and preserve it with a tablespoon or two of 50% vodka or brandy added to the mix. Generally, you can then take ¼ teaspoon up to three times a day until you see improvement of your condition. Your ¼ teaspoon can be applied to the skin over where the disease rests, or it can be taken internally, like cough syrup. You can also add the ¼ teaspoon to any cool drink you're already imbibing or to any chilled food you may be eating.

Two tips for this method are as follows: (1) if you're using stones that are raw, simply put that stone into a small jar first and then set the jar into your bowl of water. This indirect method of extracting the gem essence works just as well and poses no damage to the structural integrity of your stone. (2) If you're using an elixir or essence focused on the eyes, do not add the vodka or brandy preservative. Keep this crystal essence in the refrigerator if you need to preserve it for longer than a week.

Grid Work

While the basics of how to grid with crystals are explained in chapter 2, this section explains how to harness the energies of certain crystals in order to enact particular healing in the body, mind, community, or world as a whole. In this section, we'll walk through five types of grids that can offer solace for some more common ailments and concerns, such as heartbreak, home protection and defense, stress relief, and more.

A **Heartbreak Grid** would be composed of stones such as eudialyte, rose quartz, watermelon tourmaline, dioptase, and unakite. You would make yourself the center of this grid and lay the chosen stones around you, alternating as possible between the unakite, rose quartz, and eudialyte on the exterior of your body and holding the tourmaline and/or dioptase directly over your heart. When the minerals are assembled and, in their formation, you'd close your eyes and meditate or simply lay in their presence for anywhere from twenty minutes to an hour. You'll surely feel alleviated of your pains and ready for future prospects in a matter of days with this practice of meditation and gridding.

A **Home Protection & Defense Grid** would be composed of several stones placed inside the doors of your home or just outside them. You could use stones and minerals such as black tourmaline, obsidian, onyx, selenite, sardonyx, and carnelian to provide your protective shield. This grid would be a little different from the ones more focused on the physical body in that the crystals would ideally stay in their place for as long as you inhabit the home. Once you have the crystals and minerals you'll work with, go around your home, placing them inside each window and exterior doorway. If you only have one or two, place the stone above the door jamb of the main door you use, as possible. Meditatively place these crystals and imagine your home being protected for as long as you're there. Feel secure in your actions and know that you're doing good work.

Next, a **Stress Relief Grid** would be incredibly simple to build. You could even just use a few pieces of amethyst to complete your task. Lie down or sit in a meditative position and surround yourself with these amethyst pieces or points. If you know where you tend to hold in stress, whether it's your throat, your eyes, your hands, your heart, or otherwise, you could also place an amethyst directly over that space in your body to help. Now that everything's situated, you'd close your eyes and meditate or lay in the arrangement for about fifteen minutes, but if you really needed to detox from stress and anxiety, you could stay as long as you like. You could even arrange these amethyst points or pieces around your bed so that they're always boosting your rest with their calming potential.

A **Chakra Healing Grid** would utilize one stone of each chakra color, placed on your body near or over top the associated chakra. You could also place one brownstone for grounding at the base of your feet and one white, higher-vibration stone for ascension about five inches above the top of your head. Essentially, you would have this brownstone at your feet, a red one near your genitals, an orange one about three inches below your belly button, a yellow one on your solar plexus, a green or pink one over your heart, a blue one on your throat, an indigo stone on your third eye, and a purple one at the tip of your head followed by that bright white or clear one up top. You'd stay in this position and meditate or simply lay in the crystals' presence for anywhere from 5 minutes to an hour.

And finally, an **Immunity Booster Grid** for those with the flu or auto-immune issues would incorporate stones like emerald, brown jasper & picture jasper, green opal, rhodonite, sunstone, or zoisite from this book as well as others, such as green tourmaline, pink smithsonite, and energetic amplifiers such as quartz and malachite. You would surround yourself with the amplifiers and place the other crystals on your body. You could place the crystals intuitively where you feel they need to go, or you could focus their gathering over your throat and your heart. Once the minerals are in place, close your eyes and meditate or simply lay in their presence. After ten minutes, you could get up, or you can stay in this position for as long as an hour for a bigger boost.

Pendulum Work

If you're not sure where to start with crystal healing and you'd like more guidance than just the words I've afforded you, you might be the type for a pendulum. Across all the modalities of crystal healing, pendulum use is potentially the least-well understood, but we'll work to combat that here.

Pendulums are tricky devices. It's not so simple as taking your pendulum, swinging it between alternatives and letting it settle where it will to divine an answer. The pendulum doesn't connect with higher beings, necessarily, and it doesn't put you in contact with ghosts; not unless you ask it to!

What pendulums actually do is that they connect with your unconscious instincts. When you close your eyes and hold your pendulum completely still, you can ask it questions. Essentially, you ask *yourself* these questions, and the pendulum shows you what your unconscious self *really* wants, without those desires being cloaked by ego or anxiety or what have you.

First, you'd want to connect with your pendulum and ask it some verifiable true or false questions. Again, close your eyes and hold the pendulum completely still before you ask these questions, then ask them with confidence. After about 30 seconds, open your eyes to see how the pendulum is moving.

Sometimes, one receives "yes" from the pendulum in the form of a back and forth swing; sometimes, it's a circular motion or a complete stillness. Now try a question where the answer is "no." See how the pendulum moves after 30 seconds of your eyes being closed. Attempt this yes/no style of questioning until you're sure what your pendulum's yes and no look like.

Now for the connection with crystal healing: imagine that you'd be choosing between crystals for a healing purpose and you'd truly not know which one is best for your condition. Maybe you're unsure what your condition even is, so you're choosing between two stones you felt drawn to, but you want a more concrete answer of which is best than simply what you're physically drawn to.

In this case, you'd close your eyes and hold your pendulum still before asking, "Is the first stone (*call it by name, though*) the right one for this healing?" After 30 seconds or so, open your eyes to see the pendulum's response. Then, repeat the question for the other crystal or crystals you're choosing between. You might be surprised just how well this works for you and your process of healing.

Channeling

Some crystal healing deals with connecting to the intelligence, love, and wisdom of entities outside the earth plane. Sometimes, it means connecting to the spirits of the dead to resolve issues, conflict, or tension. Sometimes, still, it means reaching out to one's ancestors for guidance in times of great turmoil.

Crystal healing often deals with the energies of the souls that surround us. For example, we need help de-stressing from others' presences or we need encouragement to find a partner or we even need to detoxify interpersonal pollution from, say, our places of work. What's more than that, however, is that crystals can help us connect with souls that are not so obviously *material* or *physical* in order to receive overall guidance for this lifetime and beyond.

This point is where channeling comes in. For those who happen to know they're reincarnated souls from other stars or planets or galaxies, for those who happen to know that they're dealing with certain ancestors' spirits, for those who are unfortunately haunted by lingering earth souls with malice; crystal-guided channeling can be the ultimate blessing for the hope of resolution.

Through channeling stones like apophyllite, morganite, turquoise, labradorite, and more, one can meditate on these otherworldly (and occasionally supernatural) issues and receive guidance. Using apophyllite, in particular, can be groundbreaking for those connecting to entities in other dimensions or in other star systems. It's said that when you look from the base of an apophyllite crystal into its point, you open a channel for interstellar and interdimensional travel, with the right meditative focus.

Color Divination

Incredibly enough, even just a bag of crystals with one of each color of the rainbow can work wonders for those interested in divination. This type of healing connects the individual to his or her intuition, higher chakras, and higher self. Essentially, you'd choose a fabric bag that's entirely opaque and not see-through at all. Then, you'd gather up to 13 stones with any or all of the following colors: pink, red, orange, yellow, green, blue, indigo, violet, black, brown, grey, white, and clear.

Each color has a specific vibration and wavelength, due to the physics of light, which means that each color comes with a specific healing frequency and focus. For example, pink associates with love and friendship, red with passion and change, orange with creativity and growth, yellow with travel and communication, green with grounding and health, blue with sleeping and overall health, indigo with insight and guidance, and purple with spirituality and expansion.

Once you've got an assortment of stones of different colors and your non-see-through bag, put them inside and settle on a question you'd like an answer to. You can come up with a daily routine where you ask a question in the morning and see how accurate it is as the day goes along, or you could wait until the end of the day to ask guidance on how things went. Differently still, you could ask a general question whenever you like and then see what answers you receive.

Once you've asked your question, close your eyes and grab a stone or two at the behest of your intuition. With them in your hand, you can keep your eyes closed and try to sense their vibrations and then check with your vision, or you can just look to see what you've drawn. These stones and their color frequency should provide insight into your situation and somewhat of an answer to your question, and through that power of knowledge, you should find yourself one step closer to overall healing.

General Divination

With an opaque pouch filled with tens of different stones (including at least one carnelian to cleanse and recharge the rest simply and efficiently), you can try a similar divination technique to the section above with a less guided structure. Instead of asking questions for this one, you'd simply draw a stone or two to provide guidance and advice regarding life, love, work, and creation in general.

You can make yourself a list of the stones you have to work with and one or two words about each one and what it does for healing. Once you have this easy "cheat-sheet" list, you can put those stones into your non-see-through bag and pull one or two at random. Based on your "cheat-sheet," then, you will know what the stones have to say and their general advice for your situation.

You could still try asking a question and choosing stones as a means of receiving answers, but you don't *have to* use that much structure with this mode of divination. In fact, you can alter this mode of divination to suit any particular needs you might have.

For example, you could use the crystal pull of this technique to tell you something about a loved one, you could use it for help making decisions, you could use it for direction in your artistic work, and you could even use it to trigger clairvoyant visions. This style of divination is inherently flexible, and it aims to encourage your creativity, so trust your intuition and claim the sky as your limit!

Modalities of Subtle Energy Healing

Even without crystals, our abilities to heal ourselves and one another are practically endless. By laying our hands on one another through massage and surgery, we can make life-altering adjustments for people, but even without touching someone else, energy flows out in ripples that can't help but do good work.

For example, prayer is becoming more and more validated, scientifically, for its abilities to affect positive outcomes. Even without touching someone, prayer focused on any topic has positive effects at exponential rates, and the effects of prayer on the pray*er* (not the prayed-for) are healing in ways that can manifest as faith or religion but regardless, these remedies can last a lifetime.

Energy Centering, Healing, and Clearing

The more and more conscious you become of subtle energy, the easier it will be to tap into your mental, physical, and emotional health even if you have had trouble picking up on those themes in your life up until now. Subtle energy is loud for some, but for others, it's a whisper that gets bigger and louder by the day, with practice and focused attention. Regardless of where you are in your process of noticing and sensing subtle energy, there are several energetic techniques you can do to heal yours and go from there.

First, let's discuss the potential to center and ground yourself and your subtle energy. With the right application of meditative focus and healthy breathing, you can start to notice when your energy gets erratic or overly influenced by others. You can start to note when your energy gets pulled one way or the other by one person in particular, too, and when you become aware of these subtle energy hooks and interactions, you can learn how to cut loose and reground yourself in your own energetic center.

It starts with this energetic self-awareness, and then it all comes down to the powers of visualization. Once you know you need to find the center and reground yourself, it's as simple as regaining collected, calm breathing and visualizing that you have a cord that grows from the soles of your feet and connects to the earthen nature beneath. No matter how far above the soil you are, visualize that this cord can extend to be as long as needed in order to make that connection. Breathe and visualize this connection with the nature that surrounds you, and you'll be so much more able to tell what's (energetically and emotionally) yours despite any distractions or stressors.

Next, let's explore the general healing potential tied up in your subtle energetic expression. With this increased awareness of your own energetic patterns, you can become conscious of how your internal illnesses or states of disease actually ripple out, affecting your overall self-expression and energy level. While you may have always been aware of this connection between the presence of sickness and energy level, you will now be truly able to *see* the effects and their interrelation with the overall cause more clearly.

In fact, it could be that the cause of your *internal* disease was actually the *energetic* imbalance in the first place. It could be that you were internalizing, perhaps, something your parents keep fighting about or that you're taking someone's criticisms of you very personally. There are many reasons how this energetic exchange can happen, but it matters that once you know where that illness came from, you'll have the ability to change your situation for the better.

Finally, let's discuss clearing any bad or built-up energy as well as clearing cycles that could get your subtle energy stuck in a rut. Differently than *healing* your overall energy and subtle expressions, clearing something vibrationally means that you're working on just one aspect of something that's often less physical and more *meta*physical than what can be done with explicit energetic healing (like, for example, personality traits, vices, phobias, anxiety patterns, and more).

For those who notice these unproductive traits and want to do something about it, the responsibility comes in the next step. Noticing is one thing but *deciding you're ready to change* is another. Through attention to subtle energy and appreciation of how those ripples inwards and outwards work, one can accept that responsibility and approach one's own self as a canvas ready to be repainted. For those interested, you can try energetic cleansing and chakra healing to solve the vibrational issue. You can even try massage, reiki, or acupuncture to help out. Whatever you do, if you've made the decision to work out the energetic kink, be ready to shed some real-time emotional baggage, but trust that it will be for the best.

Overall, subtle energy has multiple modes of expression even just in one human body, and these techniques can help you to harness, notice, and heal that field of energy. Adding in crystals to the mix is easy to do and at some point, it will just *feel right*. For now, however, even practicing these techniques alone will be productive to your overall growth. Start with that and see where you can go.

Reiki Healing

An explicit mode of healing that's different from just subtle energetic awareness is what's called Reiki. Reiki is an ancient Japanese technique that relates back to what we discussed in the last major section about channeling, but in this case, the physical method of energetic transfer that allows one individual to *channel* energetic healing to another individual (by means of the chakras and more) to help that diseased person be able to connect with the energy of life better.

Originally, Reiki was not practiced as a massage technique whatsoever, although it has largely become that these days, with its increasingly Westernized rehearsal. It was originally just a means of using a human channel to vibrationally adjust someone else's bodily environment in order to induce that person's future healing. It still is largely this same practice overall, but the laying of hands-on skin to skin contact and the giving of massage have been added to amplify the diseased human's abilities of future healing.

Interestingly, just like the concepts of Hindu "kundalini" and "Shakti" (along with "chi," "prana," and more), Japanese "reiki" represents that life-force; giving, creative, and soulful energy of the universe. Reiki, however, is not associated with any particular religion, it simply is. Reiki work done on one another then represents this type of energy work to heal, correct, adjust, or make ready for healing anyone's vibrational essence.

Reiki healing easily aligns with chakra healing, for (as long as he or she knows about the chakras and chakra healing) the reiki healer will notice with ease and relative clarity when the individual's chakras are blocked or imbalanced. Being the energetic channel that he or she is, the reiki healer should then be able to open, adjust, clear, and rebalance the chakras by way of (massage-based or touchless) energy work. Even if this healer isn't as skilled yet in his or her work, the adjustments made on the diseased person's energy should pave the way for future progress and healing with or without the healer's additional support.

Spiritual Healing

Some veins of healing focus just on the connection one have (or strives to have) with divinity. In that sense, spiritual healing might be the right venue for people who have such interests. If you're working on blossoming your third eye and crown chakras most of all or if you're at the point where you're thinking beyond your own seven chakras out into the other 15 we have potential access to; you're doing healing work oriented with your connection to divinity. In addition, if you find yourself meditating frequently, if not daily, and if you're extra interested in aspects like reincarnation, past lives, karma, justice, or revolution, you're very likely doing spiritual self-healing work, possibly without even knowing it.

Sometimes, people are born into this lifetime thinking they'll never be good enough for God (or generally, for divinity). Some people are born with great connections to the divine that fade with time or through experiences like abuse or stifling. Some people, too, are born into this life with the potential to do great things with divinity, based on their past life careers (for example, being a shaman, clergyman, martyr, saint, etc.) but onlookers would never know otherwise.

We all are born into this lifetime with some connection to the divine, even if it's just through the fact that we're all literally *born*, coming into life through the omnipresent, creative force of the universe. Often, however, it is so much more than this simple fact of our births. We spend our whole life with proof of the divine calling out to us in multiple ways. Divinity was fractured and manifested through so many different religions and mythologies, and divinity also exists within us, for our abilities to procreate and manifest our will into existence other ways.

Divinity leaves nature as a gift for us, which we often take for granted. Divinity gives us the potential for a great feeling, which draws to us people who prove again and again that love and creativity are real and worth celebrating. Despite all that divinity does, however, some of us are more conscious, more cognizant than others, and for those who are not (or for those who experience blockages in appreciating divinity's gifts), spiritual healing is a must.

Whether one goes about spiritual healing through guided past-life meditations, attempts at channeling divinity, work devoted to relieving past-life karma, social justice work, or divinity-based educations and careers, the potential for healing is real, it is great, and it is out there. Like so many of these subtle energy healing modalities, however, it first takes one's awareness of his or her blockages and *the desire to change* before that end-goal is secured.

Ancestral Healing

Something else all of us could benefit from working on is ancestral healing. Differently, from work done on past lives, ancestral healing deals with those real-time actions our own ancestors took that put us in the places we inhabit today, in terms of one's literal home, one's socio-economic standing, one's diseases and illnesses, one's social mobility, and more. Our ancestors' actions determine so much more for us than we often imagine. They can even affect the countries we live in, the travel we have access to, and the literal meaning of our last names.

For instance, many last names deal with the trade one's ancestors worked, traced back through the male bloodline for the most part due to patriarchal naming traditions. Millers were literally that, while Browns were leatherworkers or farmers, Williamsons were descendants of a man named William, Tanners worked as leather tanners, and more. However, some last names reveal a little of what the family should be shamed for. Some last names translate back to the root of "thief" or "liar," while others like Black, Blackman, or Freeman have race-based connotations that may have been unkind.

Aside from just this naming, however, it is true that our ancestors' actions, strife, woes, successes, and advancements affect their progeny today. Sometimes, this connection we have to the past means that we live out something like a curse that our ancestors were doomed with for their faults, crimes, or flaws. Sometimes, this connection means that we live out success at the exploitation and sorrow of others. For those interested in these ancestral "hauntings" and remnants, subtle energy healing can once again come to your aid.

Through subtle & energetic dreamwork, one can attempt to reach out to one's ancestors on the plane of dreams and work out his or her connections to these long, lost dead in that way. In another way, one can use guided meditations about ancestral healing and resolution that reverberates out into peace through the generations. In another way, too, one can take on actions and responsibilities that directly *undo* the damage caused by his or her ancestors in the past.

Whether you're ancestrally aware or blind, in touch or out of touch, there may come a time when you're ready to attempt this type of subtle energetic work, and the vibrational effects in your life will be both long-standing and inspirational. However, it will take, as with this section's other techniques, a true commitment to changing oneself and a trust in one's awareness of the past; all of which crystals can greatly help with.

Trauma Healing

The more physical avenue of trauma healing also has ties to one's subtle energy field and its expression. As mentioned before with energetic healing and clearing, it can be the case that energetic wounds cause physical trauma just as easily as physical trauma causes energetic wounds. This cycle of hurt can actually bounce back and forth, creating a reverberating chamber of so-called "ripples" of hurt until lasting actions are taken.

For individuals working through trauma of any nature (physical, emotional, psychic, mental, or any combination thereof), subtle energy healing can often be of great help. Subtle energy healing comes in so many other forms than just meditation, self-awareness, and past life work. It is also imparted through herbs, essential oils, metals, and flowers that can help to boost your trauma recovery.

In the old world, herbs, oils, metals, and flowers would have been the essence and completion of any healing remedy, especially from situations of trauma. Today, we're so bent on using pharmaceutical cures that we forget how much help these old-world remedies can still be to us. While they will likely not entirely cure your situation, they will always be of help. Especially for those who are sensitive (or becoming sensitive) to subtle energies, healing done with herbs, oils, metals, and flowers can be the best body & attitude boost of all.

With the potential of herbal healing, there are a few options, of which essential oils are one. Herbs across the globe all have healing affinities. Whether they work for the blood, for digestion, for poison, or for enlightenment, herbs have always been incredibly gifted healers. Today, people suffering through trauma with PTSD and more can use herbs to make day-to-day life easier. Whether herbs are used to boost the individual's diet or to alleviate symptoms through with aromatherapies (as with incense, essential oils, and more), the herbal potential is vast and should not be taken for granted.

Metals can also be used for curative means. While metals are not ingestible like herbs or flowers, their mere presence can be strengthening and affirming. Copper is said to help with digestive, lymphatic, and immune issues, while iron supports the blood and heart. Silver works for the urinary system and fights bacterial infections. Gold strengthens in many ways, such as with memory, for cardiovascular health, with respiration, and against the effects of aging.

Finally, flowers can come into play. Certainly, the scents of flowers work an aromatherapy related to herbal healing, and essential oils exist of flowers, too. However, flowers can have their "essences" extracted in a similar way that crystals can, which provides a whole new layer of subtle energy healing. Sometimes, we're so stuck in certain ways of living that we can't imagine healing. Sometimes, we're content to wallow in disease. Sometimes, we think we're not worthy to heal, and in all these occasions, flower essences can be of great help.

These extracted and focused energies of flowers can be taken daily to boost your subtle energy in ways that make space for future healing mechanisms. Even if you're not ready to fully heal yet, for whatever reason, start taking flower essences (such as Star of

Bethlehem to alleviate soul tension and frustrations, Wild Rose to increase multitasking and end procrastination, Saguaro to enhance psychic abilities and receptiveness, and more) and after a few weeks, you'll be surprised what you're ready for in terms of healing and how much your symptoms have already been changed for the better.

How to Incorporate Crystals into Any Modality

As you go out into the world without me (as it was before me, my book, and my words), you're sure to encounter incredible and life-changing healing techniques that are ripe for a crystalline boost. In order to make you feel as prepared as possible for those moments, the following section will provide a brief guide to how you can do exactly that. The guide divides any relation between healing and crystals into a process comprised of 5 steps.

First, **assess the situation**. Take in the healing needs of the individual in question and your healing *abilities* as the individual likely approaching things as a healer (even if you're healing yourself). Think about what that healing goal will look like when it's all said and done. Think about what the situation may have been caused by and its implications on the individual's body, mind, and soul. Consider as many angles of the situation as possible to be able to develop the most intuitive remedy.

Second, **match the situation to this new strategy**. As you think of what the end-goal will look like, you will be using a new remedy or curative technique (the new healing modality to incorporate crystals into) as a potentially successful "cure." Now recall what that new cure will look like. Remember what the tenants of this new healing technique are. Think through it all, even if it's far-fetched. Think about that cure's details and just let your intuition, your reason, and your judgment work their combined magic. There's a reason why this new healing strategy was brought to you, and it might just be because it perfectly brings in line what you know about crystals and what needs to be done.

Third, **determine the strategy's weak spots**. As you think of this new healing strategy, the new potential "cure"; there will be obvious weak spots. There will be more weak spots if the "cure" is especially "far-fetched," but that just means there are more holes to fill gaps in with crystals! These weak spots are essentially that; they're invitations to tie in crystal healing. Now that you've considered the healing situation on all angles and have pondered what you know of this new strategy, look again at the weak spots and let your intuition be your guide. Some ideas of crystals or minerals *will* certainly fill your mind, and the more ideas you have, the better.

Fourth, **meditate** with the dilemma and your chosen crystals. This can look different for everyone, based on what your relationship with meditation is like and based on what crystals you actually have at your disposal. It might just look like you are closing your eyes and thinking about the situation deeply. It might be completely different and look like literal research for you. Instead, if you're practiced with meditation and have a connection with your spirit guides or guardians, you can simply ask for their advice to make sure you make the right connections for the situation.

Fifth and lastly, **fortify the strategy with crystals** for the benefit of the overall healing situation. Any case for healing has space for crystal boosters; you just have to open yourself to the possibility and do a little meditation or research to affirm your instincts. Once you have those intuitions confirmed (or altered, and that's okay too!), acquire the crystals and begin to incorporate them into your new technique.

CHAPTER 6
Advanced Crystal Healing And Details Of The Craft

When it comes to the subtle energies of crystals involved in healing or divination or what have you, there's more to it than just what I say each crystal does. For example, your intuition may be a better guide to you (eventually or now!) regarding what stones do what for which disease, and you can actually learn to guide, to hone that intuition by simply learning the "gender," elemental, and solar system/planetary associations for each stone and working from there instead.

If it's easier for you to remember what stone does what in the first place, then this chapter will just sprinkle a little extra context on top of those associations. Eventually, you will learn what it means to consider stones, crystals, and minerals with gendered, elemental, and planetary associations. You will also be introduced to the concept of crystal pairing and grouping so that you can start to create crystal healing pouches for yourself and others in need.

As one final bombshell, the end of this chapter touches on the connections between Western astrology and crystal healing. For, if each crystal has a gendered, an elemental, and a planetary alignment, surely some crystals would connect better with, say, a Pisces than a Libra, etc. We will not get into debates over esoteric astrology, the 13th sign, or other complicated astrological matters. I'm simply going to introduce you to some concepts and associations and let you decide for yourself.

By the end of this chapter, you should find your internal warehouse of knowledge on crystal healing becoming fine-tuned, and there should certainly be a few crystals that come to mind for you to begin healing yourself (and others, as your intuition and reason guide you). Essentially, you should be ready for action.

Feminine or Masculine?

To think of each stone or crystal with a gendered association does not mean to engage with debates about gender identity in the world today. It is simply to say that the universe demonstrates the existence of two gendered extremes: masculinity and femininity, and those gendered extremes are imprinted onto all life *within* that universe. This statement corresponds to the Hermetic & Universal Law of Gender, which is one of twelve that work together to define the nature of our reality.

Within humans, gendered extremes can become meshed through hormonal imbalances, gender identity, gender expression, and otherwise, but stones and crystals are far simpler than we are in this sense. The vibrations of crystals can easily align with either masculine or feminine potential, with complete exclusion of the other, and when you come to learn which stones align which way (gender-wise), you'll find that their overall energy signatures and healing potentials become more and more clear.

This universal sense of **Femininity** corresponds to passive, receptive energy. It is observant, sometimes aloof, accepting, and more subtly energetic. It hides and obscures, as well as illuminates, reveals, and enlightens. It can be sneaky and passive-aggressive, but regardless, it is oriented towards receptive interpersonal alignments and understandings. Feminine crystals are also oriented towards styles of healing that are soothing, love-related, de-stressing, wisdom-related, compassion-related, sleep-related, empowering, growth-related, and community-related.

Some **feminine** stones, minerals, and crystals are as follows: (blue, green, & moss) agate(s), amethyst, aquamarine, azurite, beryl, (blue, green, & pink) calcite(s), chrysocolla, coal, coral, emerald, fossils, geodes, jade, (brown & green) jasper(s), jet, kunzite, lapis lazuli, malachite, marble, moonstone, opal, pearl, peridot, petrified wood, (regular, blue, green, rose, & smoky) quartz(s), salt, sapphire, selenite, sodalite, sugilite, (black, blue, green, & pink) tourmaline(s), and turquoise.

This universal sense of **Masculinity**, on the other end of the spectrum, corresponds to active, forceful energy. It is assertive, sometimes demanding, controlling, and openly energetic. It presents, projects, represents and actualizes. It can be protective and defensive, but regardless, it is oriented towards forceful interpersonal interactions. Masculine crystals are also oriented towards styles of healing that are protective, intellect-related, exorcism-related, luck-related, success-related, power-boosting, confidence-boosting, courage-boosting, and will power-related.

Some **masculine** stones, minerals, and crystals are as follows: (red, banded, black, & brown) agate(s), apache tear, aventurine, bloodstone, (orange) calcite, carnelian (agate), citrine, fluorite, garnet, hematite, (red) jasper, obsidian, onyx, (fire) opal, (rutilated & tourmalinated) quartz (s), rhodochrosite, rhodonite, ruby, sardonyx, serpentine, spinel, sunstone, tiger's eye, topaz, (red) tourmaline, and zircon.

Fire, Earth, Air, or Water?

Thinking of crystals and stones with elemental associations may sound redundant to some. These people may consider that rocks, stones, crystals, minerals, etc. are harvested from the earth and should, therefore, be linked to that element more clearly than to any other. However, I wonder what these people might say about a stone-like, say, Obsidian, which is a naturally-occurring form of *volcanic glass* or about a mineral like Ammolite, which is technically a fossilized, opalized *ancient sea critter*?

Crystal healing gets complex, but it is much easier for me to break it all down into groups. The basic elemental designations are fire, earth, air, and water, and becoming familiar with those energies will hopefully be helpful for your journey with crystal healing, too.

When it comes to **fire**, the energy is associated with universal masculinity. Some minerals, stones, and crystals associated with fire are as follows: (banded, black, red, or brown) agate(s), amber, apache tear, asbestos, carnelian, citrine, diamond, garnet, hematite, (red) jasper, lava, obsidian, onyx, rhodochrosite, ruby, sardonyx, serpentine, spinel, sunstone, (regular & red) tiger's eye(s), topaz, (red & watermelon) tourmaline(s), and zircon.

When it comes to **earth**, the energy is associated with universal femininity. Some minerals, stones, and crystals associated with earth are as follows: (green & moss) agate(s), alum, (orange) calcite, chrysoprase, coal, diamond, emerald, (brown & green) jasper(s), jet, kunzite, malachite, onyx, peridot, salt, stalagmites & stalactites, (black & green) tourmaline(s), and turquoise.

When it comes to **air**, the energy is associated with universal masculinity. Some minerals, stones, and crystals associated with air are as follows: aventurine, (white) fluorite, jasper, mica, opal, pumice, (regular & blue) tiger's eye(s), topaz, and certain types of turquoise.

When it comes to **water**, the energy is associated with universal femininity. Some minerals, stones, and crystals associated with water are as follows: (blue lace) agate, amethyst, aquamarine, azurite, beryl, (pink & blue) calcite(s), chrysocolla, coral, geodes, jade, lapis lazuli, lepidolite, moonstone, mother of pearl, pearl, quartz, sapphire, selenite, sodalite, sugilite, and (pink, blue, or green) tourmaline(s).

Solar System Associations?

Crystals having solar system associations might be the wildest set of associations of this chapter for most of my listeners (and readers) to accept, but there's an easier way to explain what I mean. Of course, with the exception of "crystals" formed by meteorite debris (such as desert glass, pieces of the meteorite itself, moldavite, space diamonds, and tektite), all of the nature bits included in this text originate from Earth. The planetary or solar systemic associations of each stone are different than that.

Energetically, each crystal correlates to the vibration of a planet in our solar system or a star beyond. For example, Jupiter's energy is (through mythological associations) said to be linked to travel, expansion, higher education, spiritual studies, and luck, so the lucky abundance stone, Lodestone, relates with that energy well and clearly associates to that planet's vibration. Once you learn what these associations look like, you can intuit information and potential about a healing stone in question to determine whether it will work best for your goals or not.

The **"planetary" energy of the Sun** is about the self and self-expression, and solar healing focuses on work dealing with legal matters, general healing, protection, success attraction, literal or metaphorical illumination, and energy boosting or morale. Stones and crystals linked with this Sun energy are as follows: amber, orange calcite, carnelian, diamond, quartz, sunstone, tiger's eye, topaz, and zircon.

The **"planetary" energy of the Moon** is about emotions and self-actualization, and lunar healing focuses on work dealing with sleep & dreaming, prophecy, gardening, love, general healing, water- or sea-related healing, birth & reproduction, fertility, the home, peace, compassion, and general spirituality. Stones and crystals linked with this Moon energy are as follows: aquamarine, beryl, moonstone, mother of pearl, pearl, quartz, sapphire, and selenite.

The **"planetary" energy of Mercury** is about communication and self-expression, and mercurial healing focuses on work dealing with strengthening, mental boosting, literal or mental eloquence, divination, general studying or specific studies, self-improvement, travel, and wisdom. Stones and crystals linked with this Mercury energy are as follows: (blue lace & fire) agates(s), aventurine, jasper, mica, and pumice.

The **"planetary" energy of Venus** is about beauty and self-confidence, and Venusian healing focuses on work dealing with love, self-promotion or group promotion, fidelity, reconciliation, forgiveness, interpersonal interaction or exchanges, beauty & youth, joy & happiness, pleasure, luck, friendship, meditation, and femininity in any aspect. Stones and crystals linked with this Venus energy are as follows: amazonite, azurite, (blue, green, or pink) calcite(s), chrysocolla, coral, emerald, jade, (green) jasper, lapis lazuli, malachite, peridot, rose quartz, sodalite (pink, blue, green, or watermelon) tourmaline(s), and turquoise.

The **"planetary" energy of Mars** is about aggression and self-assertion, and Mars-based healing focuses on growing courage, building and honing aggression, recovery, physical strength, political endeavors, sexual expression, exorcism, protective & defensive work, and masculinity in any aspect. Stones and crystals linked with this Mars energy are as follows: bloodstone, garnet, (red) jasper, lava, onyx, rhodochrosite, ruby, sardonyx, and (red & watermelon) tourmaline(s).

The **"planetary" energy of Jupiter** is about luck and self-fulfillment, and Jupiter-based healing focuses on linking with spirituality, meditation, growing psychic gifts, and religious ritual in any format for healing. Stones and crystals linked with this Jupiter energy are as follows: amethyst, azurite, lapis lazuli, lepidolite, lodestone, sugilite, and (white) topaz.

The **"planetary" energy of Saturn** is about authority and self-restriction, and Saturn-based healing focuses on grounding, centering, limiting, habit breaking, protecting, purifying, and drawing appropriate luck. Stones and crystals linked with this Saturn energy are as follows: apache tear, coal, hematite, (brown) jasper, jet, lodestone, obsidian, onyx, salt, serpentine, and (black) tourmaline.

The **"planetary" energy of Uranus** is about transformation, and self-immolation and Uranus-based healing focus on guidance (for the self, the group, or both) through rebellion or transformation. Stones and crystals linked with this Uranus energy are as follows: aventurine, azurite, chrysocolla, diamond, labradorite, all quartz (esp. rutilated & tourmalinated), and (blue) topaz.

The **"planetary" energy of Neptune** is about idealism and self-delusion, and Neptune-based healing focuses on dreamwork, sleep, habit breaking, delusion-bursting, awakening, and bring ideals and goals to life. Stones and crystals linked with this Neptune energy are as follows; amethyst, celestite, Herkimer diamond, (blue & regular) howlite, jade, lepidolite, mother of pearl, sapphire, and turquoise.

The **"planetary" energy of Pluto** is about revolution and ego-death, and Pluto-based healing focuses on larger group transformation, the cycle of life, coping with death, grief, religious ritual, and general moving on. Stones and crystals linked with this Pluto energy are as follows: kunzite, malachite, obsidian, (tourmalinated & smoky) quartz(s), ruby, spinel, and topaz.

What Goes Well with What?

Now that you have a working knowledge of the associations that stones, minerals, and crystals have with gender, elements, and bodies of our solar system, you can become able to take things in your journey with crystal healing past the point of just *knowing* toward a place of *synthesis*. With this knowledge, you're at the point where you can find yourself making connections between crystals. These groupings will become essential as you progress with crystal healing, for they will allow you to actually create healing grids, make your own chakra stone set, and generally take your healing work to a whole new level.

As you start drawing these connections, and these associations begin happening for you (if they haven't begun to do so already), you have two main options. Generally, you can *pair* crystals, or you can *group* them together. The connotation here is clear: either you work with just two crystals together and focus on their energetic combination and healing potential, or you look outside a duo and begin to pull together connections and potentials for three or more allied crystals at once.

If you haven't begun to note which crystals and stones seem to go well together, we can touch on a few basics to help you along in your process first. Overall, let's start small and just look at pairings in this section before moving onto groupings in the following.

While we're starting small, think back to what you learned in chapter 2 regarding the energetic *feeling* of each crystal and how you can establish your connection to it. For just a moment, try to forget what you learned in terms of the verbose listings of the past few sections and chapters, and just go back to that intuitive sensory knowledge.

Remember how it's done? With one stone in your hand, it is relatively simple to pick up its vibration. By breathing deeply and essentially meditating with that one crystal, you get to tune into its frequency, but when you add two to one hand or hold one crystal in each hand, things get a little more interesting. They get even *more* interesting when you *do try* two crystals together and their energies feel instantly harmonious or chaotic together.

You can practice the exercise from chapter 2 again now with two crystals together. First, try holding one in each hand. See if you can tell that there are two different stones in your hands if you close your eyes. Without focusing on how those items literally *feel*, can you sense their vibration in the palm of your hand? Can you feel *more* than just that frequency, perhaps? Do you have the ability to intuit what the stone might do for healing purposes?

Regardless of where you're at with your intuition, just try to see how these stones feel. Then, you might try holding them both in one hand and intuiting how their energies are affected and altered. Do this combination and the proximity change things? Can you sense that chaotic or harmonious balance? Practice this technique, and you'll become better at it in time. There are certainly other methods to use in the meantime.

Once you've mastered or have decided to move past this intuitive connection capacity, there are two more methods you can try to see "what goes well with what." First, you can use your intuition in an entirely different way. It can certainly be said that stones that have the same abilities work well together, but stones with different yet *supportive* abilities work just as well if not better!

Go back to the index and chapter 3, go back to the sections before this (the ones with all their listings), and just read through the details again. As you read, you may realize how well certain qualities will work together, and that's exactly what I'm going for. For example, if you're trying to heal defensiveness of personality, a stone for clarity (azurite, fluorite, charoite, etc.) and one for healing defensiveness itself (red jasper, sodalite, rose quartz, malachite, etc.) may stand out to you as supportive and productive, and that intuition would be entirely sound.

Second and finally, you can let go of the intuition feature and simply do the research. Practice choosing crystals that balance one another through opposition and ones that harmonize with each other through shared intention. Put together the pairings and see what happens. Practice pairing crystals by reading around for which ones are from similar geological locations. Maybe that origin location vibration would affect healing capacity even if the stones weren't necessarily allied before!

Let the sky be the limit here. Get creative with your goals of healing, and you will easily find new crystal pairings to test out on a daily basis. If you don't have the crystals to test out just yet, don't give up! Instead, keep a journal of your findings for the future! You never know when you'll be able to come into crystal "wealth" and get to test out what you had studiously connected in the past!

How to Create Healing Pouches

When you're working with groups of crystals, it becomes much easier to look at explicit traits rather than to intuitively sense out connections, for the sheer number of crystals in the group can easily become overwhelming to keep track of even for a more experienced crystal healer. Therefore, simply look at the facts.

Gather together multiple feminine-orientation crystals for help with menstruation or menopause. Gather together several water-oriented crystals to cool you down if you struggle through hot flashes. Pull together several Jupiter-related crystals to attract luck or future travel connections. Having trouble with authority? Try meditating with some Saturn- or Uranus-oriented crystals.

Just by looking at the associations of this chapter, you can determine what is similar and how certain energies align. However, you can always go back to chapter 3 and the general index of crystals and their healing traits. You can try to pull together several stones that, for example, all work against anxiety, or you could gather together several separately-oriented stones, one for each bodily space where you need help.

When you do come to the point where you can create "pouches" of healing stones all working toward a common cause, keep these four pointers in mind. First, take into account the work the stones will do. If they're going to suck out bad energy or neutralize bad energy in any way, they will need to be cleansed more often. Furthermore, if your work focuses on explicit bodily or energetic healing, your crystals will need to be cleansed at least weekly to deal with the effort you expect them to undergo. **Basically, consider the weight of the work, and cleanse your crystals appropriately.** Otherwise, you risk holding onto exactly what you want to release.

Second, **don't overly concern yourself with "balancing" the pouch** with masculine and feminine energies, one of each of the elements, and something from each planet. There are far too many other avenues of grouped crystal healing to go down for you to stay focused on balancing something that's not your explicit healing goal. *If you really want a pouch that's constantly self-cleansing, add in a piece of carnelian.* If your focus is a compulsive balance, however, try shifting your focus elsewhere and see how your crystal grouping potentials blossom.

Third, **listen to your intuition**! If you're being drawn to crystal healing, there's surely a reason for it, and your intuition (as mentioned before) may be your greatest and most trustworthy guide of all. Let your instincts play out but do a little research after the association comes to you to see more clearly what you were picking up on.

Fourth and finally, **if you have an idea for a pouch, don't limit yourself; go for it**! This book may not provide all the answers you seek, but that's okay! Chapters like this one, in particular, are designed to ignite your ability to ask those creative and complicated questions, so don't be afraid to do additional research and to look up more statistics, details, and facts on the internet or in encyclopedias and other books. Essentially, if you come up with an idea for a pouch and this book doesn't provide helpful information for it, don't give up! Ride that intuitive wave through other sources of information until you can actualize your dream. The effort will be more than worth it.

10 Healing Pouches

This section will give you some explicit ideas of ten healing pouches that can work for a variety of goals. It should help you conceptualize what to look for with allied stones, what types of pouches are possible, and what types of healing potential exists for crystals in general.

1. Attracting Love and Growing Self-Love

    Contains: Rose quartz, amethyst, rhodonite, and tree agate.
    Goals & Intentions: To use their commonalities to boost one's self-love and romantic love capacities.

2. Technology Shield

    Contains: Aventurine, amazonite, sodalite, fluorite, and lepidolite.
    Goals & Intentions: To protect from the electromagnetic radiation that technology gives off with the combined vibrations of these crystals.

3. Fighting Depression

    Contains: Sunstone, lapis lazuli, lepidolite, rose quartz, and tree Agate.
    Goals & Intentions: To work against the imbalance of hormones that causes your depression and to reverse the effects of depression in your life.

4. Pain-Killer Stones

    Contains: Lapis lazuli, aventurine, fluorite, and amethyst.
    Goals & Intentions: To dull the sensation of, or relieve entirely one's pain.

5. Allergy Aid

    Contains: Apophyllite, lepidolite, and aventurine.
    Goals & Intentions: To assist in the relief of allergy symptoms.

6. Healing for Breast Cancer

Contains: Moss agate, bloodstone, rose quartz, rhodonite, and Moonstone.
Goals & Intentions: To relieve pain and kick-start healing.

7. To Break a Fever

Contains: Sodalite, labradorite, kyanite, hematite, and moss agate.
Goals & Intentions: To naturally cut down a fever.

8. Helper During Menstruation

Contains: Amethyst, citrine, regular moonstone, black moonstone, and labradorite.
Goals & Intentions: To make PMS and menstruation a bit easier.

9. Helper for the Upset Stomach

Contains: Turquoise, sodalite, agate, amethyst, and carnelian.
Goals & Intentions: To work against upset stomach and help restore
internal order.

10. Increased Respiratory Health

Contains: Lapis lazuli, aventurine, amethyst, and rose quartz.
Goals & Intentions: To boost immunity, aid in respiratory repair,
and help keep things flowing well with one's breath.

10 Additional Ideas

Now that you have a sense of what to look out for and what grouped stones can do together, here are ten additional ideas that you can run with if they resonate with you. If they don't, they'll surely trigger fresh ideas that *do* have meaning for your experience.

Regardless, let this section guide you and affirm your growing instincts, too.

1. Energy Booster
2. Healing Broken Heart
3. Anti-Septic Stones
4. Healing for Any Type of Cancer
5. Immunity Booster
6. Healing for Prostate
7. Memory Booster (Long-Term, Short-Term, or Both
8. Psychic Awakening
9. Diabetic Stand-By
10. Grounding After Trauma

Overall, don't limit yourself, and don't feel dejected if you can't find the information you're looking for right away! Continue striving and trust your instincts. Your future with crystal healing will surely be bright as long as you complete those steps.

Crystal Healing for the Zodiac

Without going too deep into the tenants of Western astrology, it suffices to say that each person being born at a particular time and place, under a particular zodiac sign, has a stone or set of stones that correlates to their astrological intricacies. This section will reveal its details as it goes.

Basics of Western Astrology

Within the study of Western astrology, there is more than just one sign per person. When you think of your zodiac sign, you likely think of one sign, so this may sound especially confusing for you. Essentially, what you think of as your one and only zodiac sign is actually just what's called your "sun sign." It describes the zodiac sign the sun was in the month you were born. However, you're more than just that, for the other bodies in our solar system were in other zodiac signs on the instant of your birth, and those associations affect your personality, interests, and life experiences, too.

All of these constellations, or zodiac signs, relate to planets and bodies in our solar system, too, so you can go back to the section on "Solar System Associations" to ascertain which planetary energy infuses your Sun Sign, Moon Sign, and Ascendant with the following guide:

Aries = Mars
Taurus = Venus
Gemini = Mercury
Cancer = Moon
Leo = Sun
Virgo = Mercury
Libra = Venus
Scorpio = Pluto
Sagittarius = Jupiter
Capricorn = Saturn
Aquarius = Uranus
Pisces = Neptune

In the study of Western astrology, people often talk about the "big three." The big three talks about the three so-called "biggest" astrological and astronomical influences on your personality at the moment of your birth: the monthly position of the sun (**your Sun Sign comprises your personality as others perceive it**), the daily position of the moon (**your Moon Sign relates to your emotional states, your dreams, and your impulses**), and the exact position (to the minute) of the sun, based on what zodiac constellation it was moving through the *moment* of your birth (**your Ascendant or Rising Sign relates to who you are as a deeper personality that others may not immediately perceive**).

You call this arrangement of your "big three" and beyond your "natal chart" or "birth chart." You can have your birth chart calculated online using such websites as Astro.com, Café Astrology, Astro-Charts.com, and more. Once you know at least your big three, you can come to incorporate crystal healing for every aspect of yourself. You can work on just your sun sign and its struggles, but with the aid of these websites (or simply the knowledge of your other placements), you can heal your emotional state via your moon sign and your deeper personality via your ascendant, too. The possibilities with crystal healing are limitless!

Stones for Sun Signs

Basically, **if your sun sign is Aries**, look for stones related to fiery Mars energy. As a reminder, some crystals of this nature are bloodstone, garnet, hematite, sardonyx, and red tourmaline. Some other crystals for Aries Sun include carnelian, citrine, iron pyrite, jasper, and topaz.

If your sun sign is Taurus, look for stones related to earthy Venus energy. As a reminder, some crystals of this nature are moss agate, calcite, emerald, green jasper, malachite, watermelon tourmaline, and turquoise. Some other crystals for Taurus Sun include boji stone, kyanite, lapis lazuli, peridot, and tiger's eye.

If your sun sign is Gemini, look for stones related to airy Mercury energy. As a reminder, some crystals of this nature are most agates, aventurine, jasper, mica, and pumice. Some other crystals for Gemini Sun include calcite, dendritic agate (in specific), howlite, and tiger's eye.

If your sun sign is Cancer, look for stones related to watery Moon/lunar energy. As a reminder, some crystals of this nature are aquamarine, beryl, mother of pearl, pearl, quartz, sapphire, and selenite. Some other crystals for Cancer Sun include calcite, jasper, moonstone, opal, pink tourmaline, and rhodonite.

If your sun sign is Leo, look for stones related to fiery Sun/solar energy. As a reminder, some crystals of this nature are diamond, sulfur, sunstone, topaz, and zircon. Some other crystals for Leo Sun include amber, citrine, garnet, kunzite, onyx, quartz, and tiger's eye.

If your sun sign is Virgo, look for stones related to earthy Mercury energy. As a reminder, some crystals of this nature are green aventurine and green jasper. Some other crystals for Virgo Sun include dioptase, garnet, moss agate, sodalite, and smithsonite.

If your sun sign is Libra, look for stones related to airy Venus energy. As a reminder, some crystals of this nature are yellow jasper and citrine. Some other crystals for Libra Sun include aventurine, bloodstone, jade, lepidolite, sapphire, and topaz.

If your sun sign is Scorpio, look for stones related to watery Pluto energy. As a reminder, some crystals of this nature are kunzite, malachite, and obsidian. Some other crystals for Scorpio Sun include apache tear, beryl, garnet, hawk's eye (a variation of tiger's eye), and rhodochrosite.

If your sun sign is Sagittarius, look for stones related to fiery Jupiter energy. As a reminder, some crystals of this nature are fire opal, hematite, purple flash labradorite, lava, lepidolite, lodestone, and purple flash obsidian. Some other crystals for Sagittarius Sun include amethyst, citrine, (any colored flash) labradorite, lapis lazuli, and sodalite.

If your sun sign is Capricorn, look for stones related to earthy Saturn energy. As a reminder, some crystals of this nature are coal/anthracite, jet, salt, and black tourmaline. Some other crystals for Capricorn Sun include amber, fluorite, malachite, ruby, and some tourmalines.

If your sun sign is Aquarius, look for stones related to airy Uranus energy. As a reminder, some crystals of this nature are aventurine, diamond, and mica. Some other crystals for Aquarius Sun include fluorite, labradorite, moonstone, and quartz.

If your sun sign is Pisces, look for stones related to watery Neptune energy. As a reminder, some crystals of this nature are amethyst, celestite, lepidolite, and mother of pearl. Some other crystals for Pisces Sun include agate, bloodstone, calcite, selenite, and turquoise.

Stones for Moon Signs

With Moon signs, things get a little different; the section on Solar System Associations is less of a helpful guide for these lunar placements.

For those with Aries Moon, try aventurine, bloodstone, jasper, magnesite, or sunstone. The crystal most aligned with your intuition will be Ametrine.

For those with Taurus Moon, try apache tear, green agate, calcite, lepidolite, or rhodonite. The crystal most aligned with your intuition will be Selenite.

For those with Gemini Moon, try blue selenite, snowflake obsidian, topaz, or tourmaline. The crystal most aligned with your intuition will be Aqua Aura Quartz.

For those with Cancer Moon, try carnelian, jasper, or sodalite. The crystal most aligned with your intuition will be Moonstone.

For those with Leo Moon, try ametrine, citrine, larimar, or tiger's eye. The crystal most aligned with your intuition will be Yellow Calcite.

For those with Virgo Moon, try amethyst, carnelian, citrine, or peridot. The crystal most aligned with your intuition will be Blue Kyanite.

For those with Libra Moon, try calcite, jade, larimar, or rhodochrosite. The crystal most aligned with your intuition will be Opal.

For those with Scorpio Moon, try agate, apache tear, labradorite, malachite, or obsidian. The crystal most aligned with your intuition will be Herkimer Diamond.

For those with Sagittarius Moon, try garnet, lapis lazuli, lepidolite, moss agate, or sodalite. The crystal most aligned with your intuition will be Lapis Lazuli.

For those with Capricorn Moon, try ametrine, calcite, magnesite, moonstone, or rose quartz. The crystal most aligned with your intuition will be Phantom Quartz.

For those with Aquarius Moon, try beryl, boji stones, rhodonite, or selenite. The crystal most aligned with your intuition will be Aquamarine.

For those with Pisces Moon, try aventurine, fluorite, jasper, sunstone, or tiger's eye. The crystal most aligned with your intuition will be Celestite.

Stones for Ascendant / Rising Signs

The section on Solar System Associations is once again helpful when considering your rising sign or Ascendant. **If you have Aries Rising**, look to stones with fiery Mars energy like bloodstone, garnet, hematite, sardonyx, and red tourmaline as well as the stone Jasper.

If you have Taurus Rising, look to stones with earthy Venus energy like moss agate, calcite, emerald, green jasper, malachite, peridot, watermelon tourmaline, and turquoise as well as Boji Stones.

If you have Gemini Rising, look to stones with airy Mercury energy like agate, aventurine, jasper, mica, and pumice as well as the crystal Kyanite.

If you have Cancer Rising, look to stones with watery Moon/lunar energy like aquamarine, beryl, mother of pearl, pearl, quartz, sapphire, and selenite as well as the crystal Moonstone.

If you have Leo Rising, look to stones with fiery Sun/solar energy like amber, diamond, sulfur, sunstone, tiger's eye, topaz, and zircon as well as the crystal Citrine.

If you have Virgo Rising, look to stones with earthy Mercury energy like moss agate, green aventurine, and green jasper as well as the crystal Blue Tourmaline.

If you have Libra Rising, look to stones with airy Venus energy like yellow jasper and citrine as well as the Rose Quartz crystal.

If you have Scorpio Rising, look to stones with watery Pluto energy like kunzite, malachite, and obsidian as well as the Smoky Quartz crystal.

If you have Sagittarius Rising, look to stones with fiery Jupiter energy like fire opal, hematite, purple flash labradorite, lava, lepidolite, lodestone, and purple flash obsidian as well as the crystal Topaz.

If you have Capricorn Rising, look to stones with earthy Saturn energy like coal/anthracite, jet, salt, and black tourmaline as well as the crystal Garnet.

If you have Aquarius Rising, look to stones with airy Uranus energy like aventurine, diamond, and mica as well as the crystal Amethyst.

If you have Pisces Rising, look to stones with watery Neptune energy like amethyst, celestite, lepidolite, mother of pearl, and turquoise as well as the stone Aquamarine.

CONCLUSION

As you make it to the final page of *Crystal Healing for Beginners*, you deserve another thanks. You were thanked for the download when you were welcomed to the text in the introduction, but now, it's a different story. Thank you for engaging with this text and for making it through to the end! Hopefully, it was as informative and as helpful as I intended it to be.

At this point, you should feel confident that there are ways to incorporate crystal healing into your life or daily routine, and you should have several tools at your disposal for this new and exciting phase of your life, thanks to this book. In order to achieve all the goals you likely now have for crystal healing, the next step is to take things into your own hands.

See if there are any crystals or semi-precious stones that you've unconsciously collected or drawn to you over your lifetime. See if there are any metaphysical or mineral stores in your town and go check it out! See what stones appeal to you intuitively or go with a plan in mind. Whatever tactic you use, just make sure you get out there and get started without hesitation.

Thanks again for both making it to this point and for the download! If you found this text useful in any way, please feel free to leave a review on Amazon. I can't improve without your help, and I'm also eager to know what works for you and what doesn't. Send those thoughts my way, and congratulations again!

Your future has been altered for the better through the act of reading this book, and you now have every tool (knowledge-wise) that you need to succeed. It's all up to *you* on the next phase of this journey, and I can't wait to see where you end up.

DESCRIPTION

Have you been seeing pictures of gorgeous crystals on social media and then found yourself wondering what each one was and, even more, what it did? Have you ever simply wondered what the whole "crystal healing" thing was all about? Did you know that crystals and minerals are used today for storing information, for the building of electronics, for watch-making, and more?

When it comes to crystal healing, things are a bit wild in the best possible way. It might sound crazy to think that these (sometimes very tiny) stones can heal us, but it's much more natural than you could ever imagine. In the following pages, you'll be introduced to crystal healing, its history, and its multiple modalities so that you can find the right style and technique for you.

You'll learn about...

- The statistics and abilities of over 100 unique crystals & stones.
- How to feel the energy of your crystals to begin working with them.
- How to create healing grids with your crystals.
- What chakras and crystal healing have to do with one another.
- Diagnosing & curing illness or disease.
- Reiki healing, ancestral healing, and trauma healing.
- How astrology and crystal healing correlate.
- What crystals, minerals, and stones work well with each other.
- How to create your own healing pouches of crystals.
- And much, much more!

By downloading this book, you will enable yourself to learn, grow, and heal in ways you may never have thought possible and you allow yourself to begin a beautiful adventure with crystals for the sake of incredible benefits. Every day, I thank my lucky stars for my experiences with crystal healing, and I wouldn't trade them for anything and that's why I choose to share them with you now. Good luck, and happy healing!

www.ingramcontent.com/pod-product-compliance
Lightning Source LLC
Chambersburg PA
CBHW071503070526
44578CB00001B/430